"Because we are so close .... Messiah, God's words on your lips will orchestrate the angels to overcome all obstacles in your life! Must read. Must do!"

Sid Roth, host, *It's Supernatural!*

"*The Power of Aligning Your Words to God's Will* demonstrates the true nature of prophetic ministry ordained by God and given by Jesus Christ to His Church. Hakeem Collins calls out an issue that keeps the Church of Jesus Christ from experiencing all that Jesus bought and paid for on the cross—the issue of what proceeds from our mouths. He presents the plumb line and then provides in a practical manner how we can bring ourselves into the perfect will of God by simply agreeing with Him! This book is fresh revelation for this moment in Church history, and is desperately needed to bring us into the fullest revelation of Jesus in His Church. I highly recommend this powerful work!"

Dr. Mike Hutchings, director of education, Global Awakening

"*The Power of Aligning Your Words to God's Will*, penned profoundly by Dr. Hakeem Collins, reveals the keys behind believers' most powerful force in their mouths to manifest supernatural results. This book unpacks Scriptures that will revolutionize how to align and exercise your words with God's purpose to release heaven on earth."

Naim Collins, president, Naim Collins Worldwide

"Dr. Hakeem Collins has once again authored a practical book on integrating the Word of God into our lives for breakthrough. You will learn practical keys for knowing Him more and aligning your life with God's heart. These truths will order your world, and blessings will follow."

Dr. Candice Smithyman, host, *Glory Road TV* and It's Supernatural! Network's *Your Path to Destiny*; author, *Releasing Heaven: Creating Supernatural Environments through Heavenly Encounters*

"I believe God is calling forth oracles in this hour who will boldly and unashamedly speak forth the Word of the Lord. That is why I want to endorse Dr. Hakeem Collins's newest release, *The Power of Aligning Your Words to God's Will*, as I believe it is a well-written book for those seeking to understand the prophetic power of decrees, proclamation and words."

Charlie Shamp, co-founder and president, Destiny Encounters International; vice president, Renaissance Coalition; author, *Angels* and *Transfigured*

THE POWER OF
ALIGNING
YOUR WORDS *to*
GOD'S
WILL

THE POWER OF
ALIGNING
YOUR WORDS *to*
GOD'S
WILL

HAKEEM COLLINS

Chosen

a division of Baker Publishing Group
Minneapolis, Minnesota

Published by Chosen Books
11400 Hampshire Avenue South
Minneapolis, Minnesota 55438
www.chosenbooks.com

Chosen Books is a division of
Baker Publishing Group, Grand Rapids, Michigan

Printed in the United States of America

Library of Congress Cataloging-in-Publication Data
Names: Collins, Hakeem, author.
Title: The power of aligning your words to God's will / Hakeem Collins.
Description: Minneapolis, Minnesota : Chosen Books, a division of Baker Publishing Group, [2022] | Includes bibliographical references.
Identifiers: LCCN 2021041077 | ISBN 9780800799724 (trade paper) | ISBN 9780800762643 (casebound) | ISBN 9781493435807 (ebook)
Subjects: LCSH: Bible—Quotations. | Self-talk—Religious aspects—Christianity. | Affirmations.
Classification: LCC BS416 .C65 2022 | DDC 220.5/2—dc23
LC record available at https://lccn.loc.gov/2021041077

22 23 24 25 26 27 28   7 6 5 4 3 2 1

Contents

Foreword by Cindy Jacobs   9

Part One: Aligning Your Words to God's Will

1. The Power of the Spoken Word   13
2. Power to Decree   29
3. The Anatomy of a Breakthrough   47
4. Dealing with Hindrances to Breakthrough   65
5. Unlocking Daily Revelation for Supernatural Breakthrough   83
6. Contending with God for Your Breakthrough in Specific Areas   103
7. Planning for Breakthrough Every Day   117

Part Two: 40 Breakthrough Decrees and Scripture Verses

Friendships   131
Marriage   137
Family   143
Work, Business, Career   147

Contents

Spiritual Health   153

Mindsets   159

Emotions   165

Body (Physical Health)   171

City, Country and Community   175

Finances   181

Notes   187

Foreword

The whole world came into existence through words spoken from God. Words are very important. More so if we consider that we are made in the image of God. Hakeem Collins has tapped into revelation that we need to overcome in our daily lives today.

As you read this important book, no doubt the thought might come to mind, *Why haven't I given more spiritual weight to the words I say on an everyday basis?* Why indeed?

The Bible is clear that we need to "tame our tongue." Most of us just think that simply says not to curse or say mean things to each other. But Hakeem shows us that our tongue carries a power more vast than we ever dream.

I was raised in the southern part of America. Even though I have no idea how it happened, our daily speech is full of negative things that are, at the least, not helpful, and at the most, detrimental. Take, for instance, our propensity to say things like, "Well, that just scared me to death," even though we would never really want that to be true. Another phrase is, "I was just worried sick for you!" First of all, we aren't supposed to worry, and we sure would not want to make ourselves sick over it!

Scripturally, it is clear that death and life are in the power of the tongue. Parents sometimes speak outrageous things over their children, such as, "You are just like your uncle Joe or aunt Sally, and you know what happened to them!" This is said as if being critical and comparing will spur the child on to great things! Hakeem points out how untrue this is, and even quotes the old adage, "Sticks and stones may break my bones, but words will never hurt me." But we all know that words do hurt—deeply.

While teaching us to curb our unruly and non-life-giving words, as the title of this book aptly states, it goes from the negative aspects of our speech to teaching us how to come into huge victory through using the power of words.

It is hard to believe for some, but the use of Scripture that is spoken out loud actually releases the creative power of God's Word—it is supernatural. Hebrews 4–12 tells us that. It is alive and powerful. Like a sword, it cuts to pieces man's reasoning and releases the Spirit of truth.

I encourage you to study this book carefully. It is rich in Scripture and needs to be savored, pored over and then applied. In short, it is life-changing!

You may have been searching for years to see spiritual breakthroughs in your life. Aligning your words with God's Word will miraculously see the release you have longed for. Intercessors will love this as a prayer book as well.

Be prepared to saturate yourself in this incredible book and walk in a new level of victory!

Cindy Jacobs, Generals International, Dallas, Texas

PART
ONE

Aligning Your Words
to God's Will

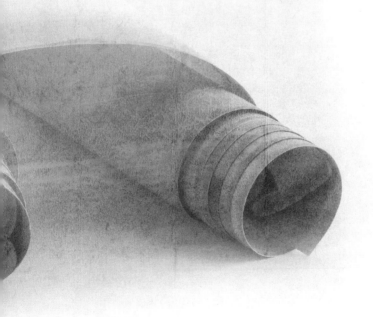

1

The Power of the Spoken Word

For no word from God shall be void of power.

Luke 1:37 ASV

There was something phenomenal that happened in the beginning of time that predates human existence. That phenomenon was the Self-Existent One—God Himself—who remarkably, unquestionably, unexplainably and sovereignly started the inception and structure of Creation with only words. His inaugural prophetic speech and supreme executive order was executed in Genesis 1, which became the cause and effect of Creation.

One of our well-known Bible verses reveals the scientific answer and absolute truth about God and the divine precedence that His Word holds. "In the beginning was the Word, and the Word was with God, and the Word was God" (John 1:1 KJV). It is clear to see by what this Scripture passage discloses that everything begins with a word.

Creative Force

This verse shares a profound message, a biblical principle, from which everyone can learn. In it is a revelation that high-lights the power of words. What we can take away from this verse is that words have power—creative power! God used words to create what He conceived in His thoughts. He spoke a command, an order in eternity past, through the means of prophetic words that were to manifest in the natural realm.

The words spoken by the Lord in the beginning of time were creative forces that were filled with faith. As you read through Genesis 1, you will notice that the words "God said" are spoken nine times. The Creator uses only words to create or form something into being. "And God said, Let there be light: and there was light" (Genesis 1:3 KJV). These words are what created the natural, or physical, realm. The world came into being, was beautifully coordinated and now exists because of the Lord's command.

To understand the biblical and spiritual principle that dictates that our words have an impact and are a creative force, we must look at a few basic definitions. The *Merriam-Webster Dictionary* defines the meaning of *words* as "a speech sound or series of speech sounds that symbolizes and communicates a meaning, a written or printed character or combination of characters representing a spoken word, or an order, command, promise or declaration."[1] The Bible is considered the *logos*, which is the written Word of God, while the *rhema* is the spoken Word of God (see Matthew 4:4; Luke 4:4, 8, 12).

Words are not just a facet of speech that roll off the tip of our tongue. Words are the most important and essential things in the universe, and they are the most powerful and creative force available to mankind. It is imperative, there-fore, to understand why that is. Words are made up of vibra-tion and sound, and the reality that surrounds us is created by these vibrations.

Words Matter

Creator God used words to create, shape and form our reality—the world in which we live. It is safe to say, then, that words are the creative force behind our world, our lives, our environment and our reality. Without the power and influence of words, our thoughts, ideas and concepts could never become reality in our lives. Research reveals that on average an individual can speak up to at least seven thousand words per day, with others having the ability to speak more words than that.[2]

Taking that fact into consideration, we must view highly the words we speak. They are important, and we must use them wisely. Words carry tremendous power and enormous influence, whether a person is a believer or not. The tongue is a potent little instrument in our mouth; therefore, we must guard it with all diligence. The words you speak daily are considered your imprint on the world.

In other words, the tongue can positively or negatively dictate how people perceive us or define us. We were created in God's image through His creative word. We have the same creative force innate in our DNA. We must be very careful, then, what we say or speak into our atmosphere. The Lord is in search of holy lives. Among those who are called to speak and live in obedience to His Word, their holy lives will be loaded with faith-filled words of right speech (see Deuter-onomy 28:1–2; John 14:15).

Words do matter, whether we want to believe it or not. Even the Lord exalts His Word above His name (see Psalm 138:2). And the Bible goes on to say that heaven and earth will pass away, but His Word will not disappear (see Luke 21:33). The power of the spoken Word of God is the source of existence of the natural and spiritual life that was created by His Spirit. The Bible shares eye-opening truths about the words we speak. It is imperative that we, as believers, understand these spiritual principles. Biblically speaking, words were the instruments by which the Lord created all things.

> By faith [that is, with an inherent trust and enduring confidence in the power, wisdom and goodness of God] we understand that the worlds (universe, ages) were framed and created [formed, put in order, and equipped for their intended purpose] by the word of God, so that what is seen was not made out of things which are visible.
>
> Hebrews 11:3 AMP

When I think about the word *frame*, what comes to mind is a picture frame that has four corners. It gives support, structure, ornamental beauty and order to the portrait that it holds. The Greek word for *frame* that was used in Hebrews 11:3 is the word *katartizō*. This means "to render, to mend (what has been broken or rent), to repair, to fit out, to equip, to put in order, to arrange, to adjust, to perfect and to complete."[3]

The heavens and the earth were placed divinely and strategically in order. They were arranged and brought to completion through God's commands. Furthermore, the power of the spoken word originates with God and those who have the delegated authority that He gave to mankind (see Genesis 1:28–31). The Lord's Word is packed with power, creative energy and life. I can imagine Him creating the universe using His words skillfully, methodically and masterfully like a carpenter who uses his tools to build something long lasting. The Lord uses His words to build and establish things. He used the power of the spoken word to create the world out of nothing. Not only did God's Word create the universe, but His Word also controls it (see Hebrews 1:3). We should view God's words as seeds that are planted for harvest.

No Empty Words

When God speaks, His Word carries out His command and does His bidding without hesitation.

> For as the rain and the snow come down from heaven, and do not return there without watering the earth and making it produce and sprout, and providing seed to the sower and bread to the eater; so will My word be which goes out of My mouth; it will not return to Me empty, without accomplishing what I desire, and without succeeding in the purpose for which I sent it.
>
> Isaiah 55:10–11 NASB

Keep in mind that if the Lord can create the world out of nothing, He can take the empty places in our lives and create useful masterpieces out of them. When the Creator crafted humans with the power of His words, He also provided them with dominion over the works of His hands (see Psalm 8:6). This dominion that was given to them was to be executed through their words.

Power, authority and influence in any area is exercised through words. When John speaks of the Word being present in the beginning, he is referring to Jesus (see John 1:2). All of creation responded to Jesus' words. He assures His disciples that creation will respond to those same words when they speak them (see John 14:12). While I have come across individuals who believe that words are insignificant or bear no responsibility, we must understand that this perspective is not backed up by Scripture. Our words have a job to perform in our lives.

Control Your Tongue

Jesus went as far as to say, "But I say to you that for every idle word men may speak, they will give account of it in the day of judgment" (Matthew 12:36 NKJV). The word *idle* means "inactive or unemployed." In other translations, the word *careless* is used. The word *idle* is the Greek word *argos*, which means "inactive, unemployed, lazy, useless, barren, and slow."[4] According to this verse, words should have a purpose when we speak them. Words will be judged as to whether they are useful or useless.

Idle or useless words are considered lazy, barren, free from labor and unproductive. The consequences of our words are weighty—even our "careless" ones. Believers must learn to discipline their physical faculties, including their tongues, and yield them to the Holy Spirit, who is the only one who can tame the tongue. "Set a guard over my mouth, LORD; keep watch over the door of my lips" (Psalm 141:3).

The apostle Paul admonishes believers about whether their words are positive or negative. "Do not let any unwholesome talk come out of your mouths, but only what is helpful for building others up according to their needs, that it may benefit those who listen" (Ephesians 4:29). The Greek word that is translated *unwholesome* means "unhealthy, unsanitary, insanitary, rotten or foul."[5] It originally referred to rotten fruit and vegetables. Being like Christ means that we do not use foul or dirty language. We need the Holy Spirit to filter our words with fresh, healthy and sanitary ones.

In today's society, some people—even believers, surprisingly—believe it is okay at times to loosely use filthy jokes, vulgar and offensive humor, and foul language. This type of language or speech, however, has no place in a believer's life. Paul admonished the Colossians by saying, "Let your conversation be always full of grace, seasoned with salt, so that you may know how to answer everyone" (Colossians 4:6; see also Colossians 3:16). As believers, we are to be transformed by the power of the Word of God.

In other words, followers of Jesus are individuals whose hearts have been changed by God's power, a change that should be reflected in their speech, word and actions. Prior to salvation, we were already judged, condemned, dead to sin and living a spiritual death (see John 3:18; Ephesians 2:1–3). The apostle Paul describes it by saying, "Their throats are open graves; their tongues practice deceit" (Romans 3:13). Our words, therefore, should consist of blessings—and not curses—due to the fact that our hearts are full of blessing (see James 3:10). And if believers saturate their hearts with Christ's love, then only purity, wisdom, truth and love can come out of their mouths (see Ephesians 5:1–2).

For this purpose, we are to use the power of our words to manifest His glory in the power of our faith in Him (see Romans 8:19; 2 Corinthians 4:6–7). "But sanctify Christ as Lord in your hearts, always being ready to make a defense to everyone who asks you to give an account for the hope that is in you, but with gentleness and respect" (1 Peter 3:15 NASB). In addition, the words we utter should display the power of the Lord's grace and the Holy Spirit's indwelling. May God equip, empower and enable us to use our words as instruments of His love and saving grace. Let us not use them for destruction, evil, division, malice, slander, false witness or dishonor.

Accountable Words

The power of our words is also governed by the power of choice. We can use them to repair as a constructive, creative force, or we can use words of despair that are destructive. Scripture emphasizes the point that we will be held accountable for what we speak in this life. It would be considered unjust if the Lord held believers accountable for their words if their words did not possess the power to do anything. Clearly, the Lord believes that our words should be active and full of faith based on what we believe and read in His Word (see 2 Corinthians 4:13).

Scripture reveals that a person's words reveal the spiritual condition of his or her heart in judgment. "The words you say will either acquit you or condemn you" (Matthew 12:37 NLT). Jesus was able to discern the heart of a person by what he or she spoke. In one instance, Jesus spoke directly to a council of Pharisees who had accused Him of getting His power from Satan (see Matthew 12:22–34). As He addressed their inaccurate assessment of Him and exposed their evil intentions, He called them a brood of vipers. "How could evil men like you speak what is good and right? For whatever is in your heart determines what you say" (verse 34 NLT).

Just as venomous snakes have a mouthful of poison, so did the group of Pharisees who had nothing but evil words to say about Jesus.

In response, Jesus warned them of the coming judgment. He told them that they, too, would be held accountable for the words they spoke (see Matthew 12:37). Just as a good tree only produces good fruit and a bad tree only produces bad fruit, a person's words reveal his or her heart condition (see verse 33). There is no better way to judge the condition of a heart than by the words he or she permits to come forth from his or her lips. Jesus offended the Pharisees when He stated, "Not what goes into the mouth defiles a man; but what comes out of the mouth, this defiles a man" (Matthew 15:11 NKJV).

Paul set the ethical standard for believers when he said, "Do not let any unwholesome talk come out of your mouths, but only what is helpful for building others up according to their needs, that it may benefit those who listen" (Ephesians 4:29). Jesus' Word is powerful, and it is filled with faith that is properly aligned to the will of the Father who sent Him (see John 6:38; 10:30; 17:21). In addition, Jesus says, "It is the Spirit who gives life; the flesh is no help at all. The words that I have spoken to you are spirit and life" (John 6:63 ESV).

Words of Faith and Healing Breakthrough

Jesus' words were always aligned to the words of the Father. He never spoke anything that the Father did not give Him to speak (see John 8:26–28). He also only did what the Father commanded, and not on His own authority (see John 12:49–50). Throughout the ministry and life of Jesus, He only spoke life-giving and creative words. The disciples and the multitudes recognized and witnessed the Spirit's power and the authority of Jesus' words through His teachings (see Luke 4:32).

When the disciples were gripped with the fear of death (see Mark 4:35–41), Jesus spoke peace to the raging sea. His words of power raised many from the dead, including the daughter of Jairus (see Mark 5:22–24, 35–43), the widow's son (see Luke 7:11–17), and His friend, Lazarus of Bethany, four days after his entombment (see John 11:38–44). In addition, the supernatural creative nature and power of Jesus' words restored a man's withered hand (see Mark 3:1–6) and healed a woman who had suffered from a spirit of infirmity for eighteen years (see Luke 13:10–17).

Also, Jesus commands two paralytic men, a man coming down from the roof on a bed and a cripple by the pool of Bethesda, to take up their beds (see Mark 2:3–5; John 5:8). The faith-filled commands of Jesus that were spoken to them healed them. It is equally important to recognize the power in the words of deliverance spoken by Jesus when He encountered a person who was tormented and possessed by evil spirits. "When evening came, many who were demon-possessed were brought to him, and he drove out the spirits with a word and healed all the sick" (Matthew 8:16).

Lastly, we can see the faith of the centurion solider who traveled a great distance to get to Jesus. He demonstrated that he understood the power and authority behind His words by asking Jesus to "just say the word from where you are, and my servant will be healed" (Matthew 8:8 NLT). He did not need Jesus to come under his roof for his family to be healed. The soldier knew that by the authority and power of the healing words that Jesus would speak, coupled with faith that created an atmosphere of breakthrough, His words would ensure that his servant would be healed, even in another location.

There is no geographic limitation to the healing power of the spoken word of the Lord. Faith activates this spiritual principle. We can see by the examples above that words that are spoken have the life-altering, resurrecting and faith-sustaining power to heal, deliver, restore and bless. This is why you should never underestimate the power of your words. The devil sure does not! He understands how words work, and he uses them as weapons against the uninformed, ignorant or faithless. Satan labors relentlessly to get God's people to turn in a negative direction.

It is the intent of the enemy to unleash a barrage of fiery darts of doubt, unbelief, sickness, pain and discouragement toward believers to cause them to speak faithless words. He knows that if he is able to get them to speak such faithless words, those words will cause them to forfeit what God has spoken. We are to only speak mountain-moving words of faith by the Holy Spirit (see Matthew 17:20). We are not to speak what the enemy is trying to deceive us into believing and speaking. Our words and faith must be aligned to the Word of God. Let's look at a couple of men who used their words to change the laws of nature.

Words of Alignment and Agreement

Take a look at Joshua 10. In this encounter, we read about how it was Joshua's faith and his obedience in partnering with God's word that stopped the universe and caused the sun and moon to stand still (see Joshua 10:12–14). In the same way, we can read about how the prophet Elijah used his words to cause a three-and-a-half-year famine (see 1 Kings 17:1).

These were ordinary men who possessed extraordinary faith to pray and believe what God spoke to them. The power of our words should always be aligned to God's will for our lives.

Make no mistake about it, your words are not powerless, useless, empty or meaningless when you host the Holy Spirit. They have innovative power, just as the Father displayed in the beginning when He created the heavens and the earth with His words. The Bible tells us that you possess the spiritual authority to do the same thing here on earth (see Ephesians 5:1; Psalm 8:5).

Start today by taking ownership over your life. The first step is to get control of your tongue. Refuse to speak anything contrary to the Word of God. Do not speak anything negative about your current life and present situation. Speak life over yourself. King David often encouraged himself in strength of the Lord (see 1 Samuel 30:6). What did he use? He used his words to do it. The ability to use words is a unique and powerful gift from the Lord.

When your words are God's words, and they are in agreement, are in alignment and are knitted with His, they do not return to you unsuccessful. They accomplish what the Lord pleases. When you and God join together by aligning your words with His will, you will prosper. Jesus said that we are one (see John 17:21–23), and we are one with Him by the Spirit (see 1 Corinthians 6:17). When your words agree with God, they become one with God. In other words, the weight of heaven endorses the words we speak when they come in agreement and alignment with His. When your words agree with the Lord's words and with His will, they suddenly supersede any and every situation you encounter. God brings His words into fruition when they are spoken in faith by those who are His (see John 3:34; Hebrews 1:3). "Then said the LORD unto me, Thou hast well seen: for I will hasten my word to perform it" (Jeremiah 1:12 KJV)

God's Word must govern your every utterance. The enemy knows that His Word in our mouth becomes a wielded weapon against the works of the enemy. The Word of God is the sword of the Spirit (see Ephesians 6:17). The Bible describes what the Word of God does. "For the word of God is living and active, sharper than any two-edged sword, piercing to the division of soul and of spirit, of joints and of marrow, and discerning the thoughts and intentions of the heart" (Hebrews 4:12 ESV). The Lord's words on your tongue dictate the rules of engagement to victory and success. The words of God in your mouth, when spoken in faith, are just as creative and powerful as God's words coming out of His mouth (see Matthew 10:20). "If anyone speaks, they should do so as one who speaks the very words of God" (1 Peter 4:11).

Words Can Hurt

Jesus, for example, only spoke and did what He heard and saw from the Father. This is what the fellowship and right alignment of our words and actions can look like as children of God. The Father has given His children the power, authority and ability to change circumstances and situations. We have the ability in Him to use our words to remove anything that becomes a hindrance to the will of the Father being accomplished. The key to a better life is determined by the words we speak. Righteous living comes by right speech. On the other hand, an unrighteous life comes by wrong speech.

The Bible tells us, "The good person out of the good treasure of his heart brings forth what is good; and the evil person out of the evil treasure brings forth what is evil; for his mouth speaks from that which fills his heart" (Luke 6:45 NASB). If you wonder whether there is really power in our words, the answer is yes. The Bible says, "The tongue has the power of life and death, and those who love it will eat its fruit" (Proverbs 18:21).

In addition, our words hold the power to build up or destroy (see Proverbs 12:6). We should ask ourselves if we are using words to build people up or tear them down. Are our words filled with love or hate, blessings or curses, compliments or complaints, love or lust, victory or defeat? Think about how others' words that were spoken to you affected you in a positive or negative way. Think about how your words have affected others.

Have you ever considered that possibly you are where you are today as a result of what you sowed and planted by what you spoke in the past? In essence, this phrase means that life has a universal principle. Whatever you do today has consequences tomorrow. This is the same spiritual law and principle the Bible teaches. "Be not deceived; God is not mocked: for whatsoever a man soweth, that shall he also reap" (Galatians 6:7 KJV). Words can hurt others—even ourselves.

You probably have heard the old nursery rhyme that says, "Sticks and stones may break my bones, but words shall never hurt me." This childhood phrase was used in defense against verbal bullying and malicious name calling. The one who was bullied tried to appear unbothered by what was said to them in an attempt to avoid a physical retaliation and to increase resiliency. The notion that physical injury is more painful than psychological or emotional injury is not necessarily true. Actually, scientific studies reveal that negative and positive words affect both children and adults on a deep emotional and psychological level. They have a significant impact on the outcome of our lives.

According to a Business Relationship Management Institute article,

> In their neuroscience experiment, "Do Words Hurt?", Maria Richter and collaborating scientists monitored subjects' brain responses to auditory and imagined negative words. During this process, they discovered painful or negative words . . . whether spoken, heard, or thought, not only cause situational stress, but also contribute to long-term anxiety.[6]

Words can influence our brains in ways that action cannot. I believe that the saying "actions speak louder than words" is untrue. This phrase states that actions are more hurtful than words. Physically speaking, actions can hurt more. But when we factor in the way words affect us mentally, emotionally and psychologically, we find that words hurt more and can be more damaging to a person's life.

As humans, our thought patterns directly shape our perception of the world and those around us. Our thoughts become our words; therefore, our language, which shapes our paradigm and belief system, establishes the culture that we speak into existence or reality. The words that we speak have the ability to put us over in life or hold us hostage to it. Even jokes with the intention of being funny can possibly tear someone down, or they can open doors to offense, anger, resentment, unforgiveness, bitterness and bad feelings toward someone.

The Bible tells us, "The mouth of the righteous is a fountain of life, but the mouth of the wicked conceals violence"

(Proverbs 10:11 ESV). There is a stark difference between the mouth of the righteous and the mouth of the wicked. There is weight upon the words that we speak; therefore, we must understand that the words we speak can become positively constructive or negatively destructive. The Bible says, "A soft answer turns away wrath, but a harsh word stirs up anger" (Proverbs 15:1 ESV).

Words spoken out of turn, in anger, in malice or in unforgiveness can create negative or unwarranted ramifications and repercussions. There are those who have been held captive in their circumstances due to the fruit of their lips. The Word of God describes words of bitterness as arrows (see Psalm 64:3) or as penetrative and venomous as vipers (see Psalm 140:3). It is clear that the tone of our words can be just as important as their meaning.

The truth is, however, that we all have problems with what we say at times. Surprisingly, James tells us that man can tame all kinds of animals, birds, reptiles and sea creatures, but he is unable to tame his own tongue (see James 3:7–8). It is clear why the Bible speaks so much about the tongue. The book of Proverbs is loaded with verses about the positive and negative aspects of the tongue. The terms *tongue*, *mouth*, *words* and *lips* are found over 170 times in the Word of God.[7]

Speaking negatively can become very costly in the spiritual realm. On the other hand, guarding our mouth and what we say can be spiritually rewarding.

Put God's Word in your heart and mouth (see Joshua 1:8). When you do, you program yourself for success and victory. When you speak words of faith daily over yourself and use them correctly, your words can make the impossible possible for you.

2

Power to Decree

You will also decree a thing, and it will be established to you.
Light will shine on your ways.

Job 22:28 WEB

*D*ecree is a biblical term that has gained popularity
throughout the Body of Christ, especially among
Pentecostals, Charismatics and Word of Faith believers who understand this principle. The book of Job tells
us, "You will also decree a thing, and it will be established to
you. Light will shine on your ways" (WEB). In other words,
Job's decision was spiritually guided, influenced and governed by the Lord's counsel and wisdom to establish Job's
ways.

His success only came because of his godly decisions that
ultimately became his destination. Likewise, believers today
possess the same spiritual authority to activate this biblical
principle in their lives. And we have the ability to decree

things that are solely aligned to God's Word to experience supernatural favor, success, divine blessings and unusual breakthroughs. Job understood the cause and effect of his decrees.

You Can Decree a Thing

Our verse in Job begins by stating, "You will decree a thing." That applies not only to Job, to prophets, to kings, to governors and to judges, but to us. As believers, we can make decrees that create things to be established. When we do, light shines on our ways. The word *thing* in the text comes from the Hebrew word *omer*, which means "the word or the promise."[1] What we are to decree, therefore, is God's Word and His promises over our lives. The Hebrew word for *decree* in this verse is the word *gāzar*, which means "to cut, divide, cut down, cut off, cut in two, snatch or separate."[2] In other words, a decree in this context is a command that not only establishes something, but it also cuts, divides, separates or exterminates something.

Biblically and historically, a thousand years before the birth of Christ, King David prophesied of the coming Messiah. "I will declare the decree: The LORD has said to Me, 'You are My Son, today I have begotten You'" (Psalm 2:7 NKJV). The verb *declare* that is used here means "to make known formally, officially or explicitly."[3] As a verb, the word *decree* means "command, ordain or decided by decree." The word *decree* used as a noun in Psalm 2:7 speaks to a formal and authoritative order, especially one having the power or force of law. It is also a judicial decision or order, and it can refer to one of the eternal purposes of God by which events are foreordained.[4] A decree is an official order that is issued by a legal authority, governing body or agent. Specifically, that order might be made by a legislating law or ordinance, or it might be an executive directive given by a president.[5]

In the United States, for instance, the president has the power of his office to issue executive orders. These are rules or orders that are issued by an executive branch of the federal government that have the force of law behind them. The major difference between an executive order and a law is in how they are created. A law must go through the entire legislative procedure and process. Both houses of Congress must approve it and later send it up to the president to be signed. In contrast, however, an executive order does not have to go through any such process.

How Decrees Are Used—Then and Now

Legally and judicially, judges have the power to issue a final verdict on a matter that requires their judgment. These decisions are synonymous with a decree or court order. Specifically, a legal decree is the decision of a court that announces the legal consequences of the facts that are found in a case. This includes the orders that dictate that the court's decision be carried out. In layman's term, it is a decision made by the order of the court that supersedes the desire or opinion of the defendant, whether it is a jail sentence, divorce finalization, a denial of driving privileges or a fine.

God has the final verdict that is in concert with His Word. His verdict is the truth and nothing but the truth! His decree cannot be changed.

God is not human, that he should lie, not a human being, that he should change his mind. Does he speak and then not act? Does he promise and not fulfill? I have received a command to bless; he has blessed, and I cannot change it.

Numbers 23:19–20

A verdict, in the legal sense of the term, is the unanimous decision that a twelve-member jury has reached in a court case. The word or term *verdict* used in legal matters comes from the Latin root word *veredictum*, which means "to say the truth."[6] God's decrees must be spoken in the truth of His Word by the spirit of truth (see John 14:17; 15:26; 16:13; 1 John 4:6; 5:6). There is power that is invested in a decree, especially when it is spoken in faith out of the mouth of God's people.

The principle that we see in Job applies to us today. What decree that we make today could become our outcome tomorrow? Perhaps what we have experienced in life could be the result of what we have decreed in the past. In Psalm 2:7, the Lord made a prophetic decree (an executive order) through King David that Jesus would be His Son. But was Jesus not already the Son of God? Was it necessary for God to speak a decree? And what do decrees have to do with believers today? If we as believers are going to understand how the Kingdom of God functions and how we were divinely created to operate in it, we must understand the power that our words have when we speak decrees.

Jesus has been present since the beginning of time. He is referred to as the Word (see John 1:1) and was with God throughout the process of Creation. The Greek word used in the above verse in the book of John is *logos*. The word *logos* refers to the entirety of the Scripture—the Bible—with Jesus being the Word of God. Jesus was the entirety of Scripture who was with God in the beginning in heaven. What was the method used by the Lord to bring the entirety of Scripture into the earth in the form of a living, breathing, speaking person? He decreed it! He spoke it. He issued His proclamations in the form of prophetic decrees. He decreed what He wanted to see happen.

Powerfully and creatively, God declared over three hundred decrees through His holy prophets in the Old Testament that foreshadowed Jesus' coming.[7] He is the embodiment of both the spoken and written Word of God. Jesus fulfilled the prophetic words that God's prophets declared. God uses both prophecy and decrees to establish His will.

God sent Gabriel, an archangel, to a young virgin woman named Mary who would be the mother of Jesus, the Messiah (see Luke 1). Gabriel declared to her, "Do not be afraid, Mary; you have found favor with God. You will conceive and give birth to a son, and you are to call him Jesus. He will be great and will be called the Son of the Most High" (Luke 1:30–32). Mary's response in faith and obedience to what the angel said was, "Be it unto me according to thy word" (verse 38 KJV). In this verse, the Greek word used for *word* is not *logos*, but the word *rhema*. This word means "the spoken word."[8] In other words, Mary spoke a prophetic decree!

Prophetic Decrees

What are prophetic decrees? Prophetic decrees are the eternal purposes, will and promises of God that are spoken and written in the form of prophecy or prediction. Prophetic decrees can also be speaking, by the authority of God, what you have heard. They declare His divine intention and His will to be done. In addition, a prophetic decree may be a declaration that is inspired by the Holy Spirit and made in faith that causes those things that are nonexistent to exist. A decree may come in the form of an announcement or a commanding order.

When we decree something in the name of God, we are making a declaration that has the weight of heaven and God's delegated authority behind it. We are to decree God's Kingdom to come, His will to be done, on earth as it is in heaven (see Matthew 6:10). We are to bind and loose with the authority given to believers to enforce God's will in the earth (see Matthew 18:18).

Believers must understand that a prophetic decree is not a formula, template or one's point of view. It is God's standpoint and point of view through His Word. In other words, our decrees become prophetic when they are sourced in our heavenly Father's will. The agency of the Holy Spirit must reveal the Lord's will to us.

Keep in mind that believers have been given the power to declare and decree by commanding their day (see Job 38:12). We will talk more about commanding our morning in the last chapter, but for now, we must be confident in knowing that it is our Kingdom duty to decree prophetically God's promises in the earth. When we do this, the Father in heaven can take His words that are spoken out of our mouths and make them become flesh in our lives.

God's words are settled first in heaven, but they do not get settled in the earthly realm until we speak them. Our prophetic decrees possess the power to unlock the resources of the Kingdom, to touch and mend broken hearts and to heal. They have the power to change atmospheres and to break through demonic resistance, strongholds and unseen opposition. They can shift situations and circumstances to bring them into alignment with God's purposes. Prophetic decrees are more powerful when they are announced.

According to the Word of God, a decree is a royal command. A royal decree was followed by the proclamation or announcement of whatever was decreed. It was not enough that a king, emperor or governor made a decree—that decree had to then be published and conveyed throughout all of the kingdom or empire. A decree and proclamation are part of a two-step process, and they serve a dual function.

Power behind Words

A proclamation is an announcement of a decree. It is a vital part of the process to have the wishes of a king or a ruler become reality. Knowledge of the decree permits individuals to proactively respond and position themselves to be in obedience with what is announced or proclaimed. Also, there is power in a decree, even when it is utilized in private prayers, intercession and times of worship with the Father. Leaders must understand the necessity and importance of the power of public, prophetic proclamation.

It is not about using the word *decree* as part of a formula that brings the power to the declaration, but rather understanding one's spiritual authority and right to make the decree. In other words, prophetic decrees should flow organically and naturally when we comprehend and speak them from our heavenly position on earth (see Ephesians 2:6). The power is not in the mere words we use, but in the revelation and authority that is given to us as co-heirs in His Kingdom through Christ Jesus.

A prophetic decree is potent when it flows from the acknowledgment and revelation that we have been made priests in His Kingdom to carry God's kingly authority and serve His eternal will (see Revelation 1:6). God uses ordinary people to speak extraordinary things. He wants to use your voice and tongue to speak His decrees. He uses people to speak forth His divine commands (decrees). We are to be His submitted agents who declare on earth what the Father has already established in heaven.

A prophetic decree becomes powerfully creative when we speak it as the Lord did. He said, "Let there be" (Genesis 1:3). Jesus understood the power of alignment and prophetic decrees spoken to Him in prayer by the Father. He only spoke, decreed, repeated and demonstrated what He saw and heard from God (see John 5:19; 8:38; 12:49–50). We see the power in verbalizing and why it is so important in the relationship between Jesus and God. After the Father called Jesus His Son (see Psalm 2:7), He then told Jesus to speak. "Ask of Me, and I will give You the nations for Your inheritance, and the ends of the earth for Your possession" (Psalm 2:8 NKJV).

The Father's will for His Son and His followers was that they would disciple whole nations. Those nations were Jesus' inheritance; however, it was not automatic. Jesus Himself had to issue a decree. In Psalm 2:8, the word translated to *ask* means "to inquire, to request, or to make a demand on."[9] It means to ask assertively with expectancy. Likewise, as believers we can go boldly before God in prayer to ask whatsoever in Jesus' name. We are told that we will then receive what we ask for according to His will (see John 14:14; 16:24).

When we make a prophetic decree, we should not speak our own personal desires or wish lists of things we would like to see fulfilled. We are to be making an assured declaration of our Father's revealed intention. Those intentions are revealed to us in the secret place in prayer in God's presence.

The power to decree is not new terminology, nor is it new age ideology. It is a biblical principle, concept and revelation that originated with the Lord. This phraseology and theology started with God. As King, Ruler and Creator of the universe, His first decree was what He spoke in the beginning. "God said, 'Let there be light,' and there was light" (Genesis 1:3). When God makes decrees, the natural realm obeys.

A King's Decree

The Lord's words are not only declarative, but they are causative as well. When the Lord created mankind, He gave us dominion over His creative works in the earth (see Psalm 8:6). He provided mankind (male and female) with royal and regal responsibilities by the weight of His decrees that set things in motion.

Decrees have been around and used for thousands of years by kingdoms, institutions, governments and empires as a means to deliver and carry out judgments, laws and orders. The power to decree is not limited or exclusive to those who were kings, rulers of nations, emperors, judges, Bible figures or prophets.

Today, all who follow Jesus and are ready to exercise Kingdom authority have available to them the power and the right to issue a decree. This is done by the Holy Spirit for the purpose of advancing the Kingdom of God. The books of Daniel, Esther, Ezra, Job, Exodus and Psalms are about decrees that were issued that transformed the course of history.

A king rules and governs by his decrees, while his citizens are to live by and obey them. Whether a decree is spoken or written, it is announced to others for the purpose of being carried out. A king's decree, order or edict becomes constitutional in his domain or sphere of rule, and it is received as law to the people. A king's decree is firm and unchangeable (see Daniel 2:5). A decree in the historical and biblical context would be considered the law. When a king speaks, his subjects must pay attention and obey instantly.

As we declare the Father's will through a prophetic decree, the unseen realm pays attention instantaneously and comes into alignment with the angels of God assisting. "Praise the LORD, you angels, you mighty ones who carry out his plans, listening for each of his commands" (Psalm 103:20 NLT). The book of Hebrews tells us, "Are not all angels ministering spirits sent to serve those who will inherit salvation?" (Hebrews 1:14).

This is how miracles, healing, signs and wonders break into the natural (physical) realm. You have the authority to speak words that move mountains, shake kingdoms and make hell tremble (see Mark 11:23). God declares, "By me kings reign, and princes decree justice. By me princes rule, and nobles, even all the judges of the earth" (Proverbs 8:15–16 KJV).

Because of God's enduring love for His people, He was pleased to place King David on the throne. As king, David's job was to carry out judgment and justice (see 1 Kings 10:9). Godly kings were in power not to carry out their own will by decrees, but they were to rule in wisdom justly, fairly and righteously in the fear of the Lord. The Lord's decrees were executed through justice and judgment in the life of His people. The Bible declares, "Where the word of a king is, there is power; and who may say to him, 'What are you doing?'" (Ecclesiastes 8:4 NKJV). The New Living Translation puts it like this: "His command is backed by great power.

No one can resist or question it." We can see the power in a king's decree.

The Old Testament tells us that the Lord never intended for Israel to have a king as other nations did. He intended to be their King. When they cried out for a king to rule over them, He granted their request and selected one for them (see 1 Samuel 8). Saul was Israel's first king. It is the Lord who sets up and removes kings from their positions of power (see Daniel 2:21). Consequently, through the act of disobedience to the Lord's decree, God unseated Saul and chose another king for Israel. This time, He chose David, who was a man after His own heart (see 1 Samuel 13:14).

God's Decrees

We must keep in mind that all authorities are placed by God (see Romans 13:1). He places all rulers, presidents and people who are in power and authority in their positions of leadership, and He works in their hearts to fulfill His will and purpose. He has prompted decrees from them throughout the history of the world. God's Word is undisputed, and His decrees are infallible!

When Israel and Judah were falling into idolatry, for example, God rebuked them. He spoke through the prophet Jeremiah and said, "The LORD Almighty, who planted you, has decreed disaster for you, because the people of both Israel and Judah have done evil and aroused my anger by burning incense to Baal" (Jeremiah 11:17).

Another example is when the Lord gave Moses the Ten Commandments. He met with Moses on Mount Sinai to pass on the commandments so that Moses would give them to His people (see Exodus 24:12). The Law of Moses was given by God to His people to obey (see Exodus 20:1–17; Deuteronomy 5:6–21). They were God's decrees to maintain order and His conditional covenant between Him and His people.

You may have heard believers say that we only have the biblical authority to pray for His will to be done but not to decree things for God. This, however, contradicts what Scripture teaches. Job tells us, "What you decide on will be done, and light will shine on your ways" (Job 22:28). And Matthew says, "For by your words you will be acquitted, and by your words you will be condemned" (Matthew 12:37).

Spiritually and practically, a decree is taking God's words and speaking them out. God has given every follower of Christ the power to activate His will through decrees so that we may overcome any obstacle we may face. We do this by vocalizing His Word. And as we do it, we begin to see His promises and divine purposes unfolding and manifesting from the spiritual into the natural. I love what Proverbs declares: "Many plans are in a man's heart, but the LORD's decree will prevail" (Proverbs 19:21 HCSB).

Decrees have the ability to change a person's beliefs if they are rooted in the Word of God. "The decision is announced by messengers" (Daniel 4:17). Some matters are determined or decided upon by God's people speaking declaratively and giving voice to decrees that alter, shift and align heaven's agenda on earth. This can happen when we agree and announce them.

What a person believes about themselves, the world and their circumstances ultimately creates their reality. This is true whether they want to believe it or not. There is life and death in what we speak or decree (see Proverbs 18:21). People have the power to create what they believe (see Matthew 15:18).

It is important to note that as believers, we create our decrees based on God, the highest power that exists. There is nothing greater that could possibly overturn, veto or recall it. Throughout the Old Testament, the Lord consistently issued decrees of blessings upon those who were obedient (see Deuteronomy 28:8). He issued decrees of judgment against the disobedient (see 1 Kings 2:27; Isaiah 31:2). And He issued a divorce decree against Israel for unfaithfulness to Him (see Jeremiah 3:8). He also issued a covenantal decree upon those who were His (see 1 Chronicles 16:15–17).

A Royal Decree Made

David, Solomon and Cyrus were kings who established royal decrees. Throughout the book of Ezra, King Cyrus issued royal decrees to rebuild the temple at Jerusalem (see Ezra 5:13). Cyrus's decrees were backed up with royal resources, and the proclamation of those decrees unlocked the power of generous giving and the manpower of volunteer work (see Ezra 1). During the reign of Xerxes, the king of Persia, a genocide type of decree was issued. It declared that all Jews were to be killed. This was accomplished through the wicked recommendation of Haman, the king's power-hungry and jealous prime minister. According to Persian customs, decrees were deemed irrevocable.

No one, including the emperor himself, could recall, revoke or remove it. Decrees are irrevocable! It appeared as if all hope was lost for the Jews because of this horrible decree. By the intervention of the Lord's providence, however, the Jews were ultimately spared from this slaughter (see Esther 8:10–14). Surprisingly, a second decree came to reverse the king's original one that had been published throughout the empire. This new decree declared that the Jews were permitted to protect themselves from their enemies.

This new decree served as a way of escape for the Jews. Queen Esther played a pivotal role in securing the new decree. Her decree served as an indictment of charges against Haman so that the negative fate of the Jews was no longer inevitable. They recognized the power of a decree to destroy them and the power of a decree to save them. These two proclamations came from the same king. Moreover, King Hezekiah established a decree that called for all of Israel and Judah to participate in corporate repentance, and he invited them to Jerusalem for the Passover.

His decree sparked a national revival that caused the multitudes to turn their hearts back to the Lord as they celebrated the Passover for the first time in generations. Later, this event resulted in the mass destruction of pagan altars, or "high places," that had been dedicated to false deities (see 2 Chronicles 30–31). There is power in the decree you speak when you align your words with God's will.

Unfortunately, there are some Bible teachers who make the argument that this type of practice is a "decree and declare" movement. It is also often called a "name it and claim it" formula. They believe it is false doctrine and charismatic manipulation, and those who practice the power to decree are positively confessing anything that comes to their minds using bold and authoritative verbiage along with certain words to manipulate and bring their agenda to pass. Their perspective on this topic of decrees, faith confessions or declarations is far from the truth. The Bible says that we are to call those things that are not as though they are (see Romans 4:17).

The Power and Result of a Decree

What happens in the invisible realm when decrees are released in prayer by believers? They become like stealth bombers dropping air strikes over enemy territory. Stealth aircraft were designed specifically to penetrate through enemy defenses to secretly carry out strategic warfare assignments. They were built to travel very fast to intercept the enemy's plans and to catch them unaware. One distinct function of stealth bombers is their incredible ability to remain virtually undetectable by radar while carrying out long-distance strikes against the enemy.

Decrees operate in the same manner. They create breakthroughs for believers in both the spiritual and natural realms. Decrees have the power to send the enemy into confusion and fear. He has no ability to anticipate decrees, and therefore has no capacity to formulate a last-minute plan of counterattack.

Satan does not know what will be decreed. He does not know when, where or how the decree missiles are going to strike. If God's people incorporate in their decrees the proper use of Scripture, then they are able to interfere in the evil plans of the enemy. You can, for example, prophetically decree something such as this: "Father, I decree today according to Luke 10:19 that You have given me supernatural breakthrough power to tread on serpents and scorpions and over all the power of the enemy. Nothing shall by any means hurt me in Jesus' name."

It is vitally important for God's people to daily vocalize bold decrees of God's Word. When believers align their words to God's promises and prophetic decrees, those words will not fail. It is powerful and assuring to know that it is God who will see to it that His decrees will come to pass.

What a Decree Is Not

Let's look briefly at what a decree is not. Decreeing things is not a prophecy, and a prophecy is not a decree, so to speak. Making a decree is simply restating God's will and promises. Prophecy at its most basic biblical definition is a message inspired by God, a divine revelation. The Bible says that prophets "spoke from God as they were carried along by Holy Spirit" (2 Peter 1:21). To prophesy is to proclaim a message from God that brings edification, exhortation and comfort (see 1 Corinthians 14:3).

Moreover, a declaration is not a decree. To declare something means "to make known, set forth, or state clearly, especially in explicit or formal terms or announce officially or proclaim."[10] When we look at the word *command*, we see that it is a part of a decree; however, anyone can command something. Not all are authorized to decree. To command means "to give an order; direct; charge; implying authority, and power to control, and to require obedience."[11]

Prayer is not a decree either, even though we hear God's will in prayer. Prayer is the primary way for believers in Jesus Christ to communicate their emotions and desires with God and to be in fellowship with Him. Prayer can be audible or silent, private or public, formal or informal. All prayers must be offered in faith (see James 1:6), in the name of the Lord Jesus (see John 16:23) and in the power of the Holy Spirit (see Romans 8:26).

We also must look at the process of confession. Confession is a statement of fact and truth, but even though a decree is truth, a confession is different from a decree. A confession is an admission, declaration or acknowledgment of truth (see 1 John 1:9; James 5:16). Decrees should be spoken about what God has written in His Word.

Unfortunately, in the Body of Christ, words can be misused as witchcraft. Any form of words spoken with the intent to cause bodily injury or harm is not a decree but a curse or witchcraft. These should not be practiced by believers.

Lastly, a decree is not demanding or fleecing God to bend to what we want Him to do. Declaring a decree is not thinking God will back up whatever we name and claim or blab and grab. This practice is not biblically supported. Decreeing, declaring, prophesying and confessing the truth and promises of God, however, are biblical.

Decrees are for the responsible believer who understands when and how to use them to receive spiritual breakthroughs. The practice of making decrees finds its precedent throughout both the Old and New Testaments. The spiritual exercise and practice of it is simply vocalizing and reminding God of what He said in His promises. It is assuring God that you know His promises and are speaking them forth in faith. This process should happen with the Holy Spirit's boldness in any circumstance and situation.

God's commandments, orders or decrees were a part of His covenant conditions, and that has not changed, even for New Covenant believers today. Jesus said, "If you love Me, you will keep My commandments" (John 14:15 NASB). He followed that up with, "If anyone loves Me, he will follow My word; and My Father will love him, and We will come to him and make Our dwelling with him" (John 14:23 NASB).

It Is Written

Jesus understood not only the power of words spoken but the power of written decrees as the Word of God when Satan came to tempt Him in the wilderness. Keep in mind that

Satan thoroughly knows the Word better than most believers today. He intentionally misquoted Scripture in order for Jesus to violate the technicality of God's law and to become a law breaker. In three temptation attempts, Satan fails to persuade Jesus to break any of God's written decrees.

A powerful first response to Satan's temptation was when Jesus said, "It is written, 'Man shall not live by bread alone, but by every word that proceeds from the mouth of God'" (Matthew 4:4 NKJV). Jesus was saying that man lives not only by the written decrees of God's Word (*logos*), but also by every spoken decree out of the mouth of God (*rhema*). Decrees can be either spoken or written. The devil cannot stand someone who knows and lives by the code of the Word of God.

Decrees are more powerful than just words recklessly, ignorantly or loosely spoken. They are supernaturally purposeful, and they carry meaning. When we decree God's words, they become a beacon of light that gives us clear direction toward our destiny in times of uncertainty (see Psalm 119:105–106). The power to decree is a biblical right, inheritance and privilege for all believers. His decrees are eternal!

Success and spiritual breakthroughs come when believers decree, obey and accomplish the Lord's will in their lives daily. Christ will reveal Himself to those whom the Father will love (see John 14:21). Paul assures us, "He made known to us the mystery of His will, according to His good pleasure which He set forth in Him" (Ephesians 1:9 NASB). It is one thing to know God's will, but it is another to fulfill it. God's will—His decrees—are made known to those who will seek Him for them.

3

The Anatomy of a Breakthrough

The Word became flesh and made his dwelling among us. We have seen his glory, the glory of the one and only Son, who came from the Father, full of grace and truth.

John 1:14

God's voice and the words He speaks are the most powerful forces in the universe. He gave voice to words that became creatively supernatural in the beginning of time (see Genesis 1). He has granted His people the same creative power and mandate so that we can declare what He speaks through the Holy Spirit—to say what He says, or to say it as He would say it (see Matthew 11:23; 1 Peter 4:11).

Hearing God's voice and speaking exactly what we hear is powerfully prophetic in nature (see Deuteronomy 32:1–2; Isaiah 30:21). Our tongues and voices become a superpower through God's Spirit. We are as powerful as we allow our voices and words to be. When they are spoken in truth through God's Word, they are equally potent.

Our words, therefore, should always align with His Word, which is a part of the anatomy of breakthrough that comes through the Body of Christ. The Lord's voice is the sounding board of breakthrough from heaven to earth (see Isaiah 55:11). The Bible says that "nations are in uproar, kingdoms fall; he lifts his voice, the earth melts" (Psalm 46:6). The time period from the book of Malachi to the book of Matthew (Old to New Covenant) was considered the silent years. For four hundred years, the Lord did not utter a word to His people.

Power through the Voice

Suddenly, a new dispensation was arising, and the introduction of a new era started to spring forth. God decided to break His silence by using the rare voice of a strange-looking harbinger by the name of John the Baptizer. He was referred to as a voice of one crying aloud in the wilderness (see Matthew 3; Mark 1:3–5). He was a prophetic forerunner, reformer and truth teller who was needed in his generation. He was called to "turn the hearts of the parents to their children, and the hearts of the children to their parents" (Malachi 4:6).

John was considered *a voice* in the wilderness, which was an expression used to denote an unpopular message. That phrase referred to ideas that opposed the fashion of the time. His voice was used and called to speak truth to those who were in power in his day. His was a lone voice pleading against the action being taken by the majority. That voice became the bridge from the old to the new, and it ushered in a new spiritual era and awakening as the "kingdom age."[1] "Later, John the Baptizer appeared in the desert of Judea. His message was, 'Turn to God and change the way you think and act, because the kingdom of heaven is near'" (Matthew 3:1–2 GW).

He heralded a message of change and repentance (see Matthew 3:1–8). He was not the Voice *per se*, but a prophetic voice used of God to bring Kingdom reformation and spiritual alignment. In contrast, Jesus was the Voice who ultimately brought us back into right relationship with Abba Father through His blood (see John 10:9; 14:6; Hebrews 10:19–22; Colossians 1:19–20).

The message of John and Jesus brought alignment to the hearers. Their message brought either a negative or positive response (to reject or accept) regarding God's truth and invitation of reconciliation. The Gospel is the power of God unto salvation (see Romans 1:16). In fact, the Gospel contains the essence of God's ability, force and power. There is a supernatural force of breakthrough and creativity in the words we give voice to and in what we hear and receive as truth. God's Word is life-changing when we believe and receive it in our hearts. Jesus says, "The words I have spoken to you—they are full of the Spirit and life" (John 6:63).

His words are infused with supernatural power and an unseen force. If believers receive by faith the words that are spoken, those words will start to work in their lives. The words will begin to produce what the Lord intended them to produce. We become more like Christ when we become one with His Word. Jesus demonstrated the works that the Father sent Him to do on earth (see John 5:17; 10:37).

God works His Word through us when we align ourselves with, agree to obey and announce His will over our lives by faith in prayer. Jesus worked His Father's business and never deviated from it. At twelve years old, He understood instinctively that He was to be about His Father's business (see Luke 2:41–52). The Father's work became the Son's work to finish (see John 4:34).

In other words, Jesus came into divine agreement and alignment with what He heard and saw the Father do in prayer through the Spirit. Likewise, believers are to do the work of the Father. We accomplish this by the supernatural power of God through the Holy Spirit working in us to fulfill His will here and now. Jesus said, "My Father has been working until now [He has never ceased working], and I too am working" (John 5:17 AMP).

In every generation, God looks for willing and obedient individuals who will partner with His Word, will and promises to fulfill them in the earth (see Isaiah 1:19–20). Obedience is very important to the Lord. He wants His children to adhere to His words daily. The general concept of obedience, both in the Old and New Testaments, relates to hearing or hearkening to a higher authority than oneself. The Bible conveys one of the Greek terms for obedience. It is the biblical concept of positioning oneself under someone by submitting to their command, rules and authority. In addition, in the New Testament you will find another Greek word for *obey* is *peithō* and means "to listen, obey, yield to, comply with, trust, have confidence and be confident."[2]

Words of Life

According to the *Holman Illustrated Bible Dictionary*, a succinct definition of biblical obedience is "to hear God's Word and act accordingly."[3] The power of God's Word brings restoration, reconstruction, revival and reformation when released in God's timing. The Bible shares the power of prophetic decrees that are spoken in obedience in the valley of dry bones (see Ezekiel 37). God utilized the power of prophecy to bring national restoration and revival to a people who had lost all hope. It was the strength in the Word of the Lord that was spoken out by Ezekiel who believed that God could resurrect what appeared to be a dead army. He trusted that God could raise up this mighty army supernaturally.

Ezekiel had to perceive and believe what God was showing him, which was from God's perspective and point of view. Once he believed and perceived what God was showing him in the vision, he was used instrumentally to prophesy Israel's restoration. He had to align his heart with the Lord's heart to be able to speak to dry bones in order to see them become a living, breathing family of God.

Faith is connected to our obedience. Hearing develops our faith so that we are able to discern God's voice in prayer. Ezekiel was shown a vision, and he was used by the Lord to prophesy to the anatomy of lifeless, dry bones to see the reconstruction of a chosen generation's rebirth. Obedience is better than sacrifice when we align our hearts with God's heart (see 1 Samuel 15:22).

More importantly, I believe God is looking for faithful men and women He can call His friends as He did Abraham. Abraham was the only one mentioned in the Bible who was considered a friend of God. His faith and total obedience in what God instructed him to do was what God looked for in a companion (see 2 Chronicles 20:7; Isaiah 41:8; James 2:23). Jesus called Lazarus His friend (see John 11:11), and He calls all who believe on Him and obey Him friends (see

John 15:15). As His friends, we can share His love and fellowship, and we can know His will.

We have access to become God's most trusted confidants. The Word of God depicts a true friend as an individual who sticks closer than a brother (see Proverbs 18:24), and who is constant in their friendliness, loyalty and accountability. A friend comes to the aid of his or her companion in times of distress, and he or she speaks the truth when giving counsel (see Proverbs 17:17; 27:6, 9). True friends support and believe in each other's visions. They also share common interests, and they keep each other's secrets. Jesus considers His family to be those who do the will of God (see Mark 3:35).

The Lord wants to bring healing, deliverance, miracles, signs and wonders and financial breakthrough to His Body, the Church. The natural body only responds to what the brain signals for it to do. Jesus is the Head of His Body—the Church; therefore, the spinal cord of the Body of Christ, spiritually speaking, must be aligned to the Head in order to experience mobility. Will you align yourself, your words and your actions to God's will with your faith and obedience? God blesses those who are obedient (see Luke 11:28).

The Bible tells us that we can encounter the unmeasurable favor of the Lord. "If you fully obey the LORD your God and carefully follow all his commands I give you today, the LORD your God will set you high above all the nations on earth" (Deuteronomy 28:1). Aligning, agreeing and obeying God's will brings divine blessings from the Father. Consequently, disobedience brings curses (see Deuteronomy 28:15). Our spiritual breakthrough is predicated upon whether or not we will obey God. Obedience and faith are the culture of the believer in the Kingdom of God.

The anatomy of a breakthrough comes only through the reality of faith in the life of the believer. It is the will of the Father that we are called not only to fulfill His will for our lives but also to walk out in faith our divine calling and purpose. We must not only understand God's Word, but we must know His will for our lives. He fulfills that purpose in us through the work of the Holy Spirit. "I cry out to God Most High, to God who fulfills his purpose for me" (Psalm 57:2 ESV).

It is imperative that you pray and seek the Lord's purpose for your life daily. Your days are numbered by the Lord (see Job 14:5). He asks you to fulfill every one of the purposes He has for you; however, it is our decisions, actions and life-altering choices that also matter. Our decisions can alter God's overall destiny and plan for our lives if they are not aligned completely to His perfect will. He has given us free will in life, but those who choose to align themselves with God's will and purpose will live victoriously and prosperously! Let's look at key elements of a supernatural breakthrough.

Obedience to God's Word

Oftentimes, we become so focused on fulfilling our own plans that we forget the purpose behind them. We must have the mentality that Jesus had at the Garden of Gethsemane. He faced fear and trepidation as He anticipated the unbearable suffering He would experience on Calvary's cross. He prayed to the Father for strength to do His will. Nevertheless, He made the decision to fall on His knees to pray these words, "Father, if you are willing, please take this cup of suffering away from me. Yet I want your will to be done, not mine"

(Luke 22:42 NLT). Jesus did not allow fear to overwhelm Him or thrust Him into despair. He aligned His heart's posture to the Father's will, even unto death on the cross.

Jesus realized and understood this was His purpose. He knew that fulfilling all righteousness and destroying the works of the devil was why He was sent to the earth (see Mark 3:15; John 3:16; 1 John 3:8). As a child, He had learned obedience by what He suffered (see Hebrews 5:8). Jesus had eighteen years, between the ages of twelve to thirty, during which He had to align, agree and understand His purpose and calling as the Son of God. We, too, must go through our own spiritual process of maturation and development in our relationship with God.

Learning and trusting in God, however, is not an overnight process. The Helper—the Holy Spirit—inside each of us will empower us to overcome any and every unseen obstacle that is in the way of our breakthrough. Everyone has been given an innate purpose by God at birth. His divine purposes, plan and will for our life not only encompass us personally, but the lives of those who are within our sphere of influence—work, community, home, school, business and church. "But I have raised you up for this very purpose, that I might show you my power and that my name might be proclaimed in all the earth" (Exodus 9:16). This verse is vital for every believer. We must understand it and live it out as God's purpose works through us.

The Body of Christ becomes the place where God uses every member of it to fulfill various supernatural functions (see Romans 12:4–5; Ephesians 5:29–30). The anatomy of the Body of Christ must operate in faith to speak and obey God's will—His Word. Faith is the prerequisite for standing in right fellowship and relationship with God. We cannot please Him without faith. It will require supernatural faith to receive supernatural spiritual breakthroughs.

Faith-Filled Words

My spiritual papa, the late Bob Jones, a seer and a prophet, used to say to me, "If I want to receive everything the Bible says, I must believe and obey everything it says." This kind of faith only comes when we read and know God's will through His Word. "But without faith it is impossible to please him: for he that cometh to God must believe that he is, and that he is a rewarder of them that diligently seek him" (Hebrews 11:6 KJV). What is faith? Faith is what comes by hearing God's Word (see Romans 10:17). If we are going to align our words with God's will, then we must first agree to build our trust and sole reliance on it—no matter what. Spiritual blessings and breakthroughs are only accessed through a measure of faith (see Hebrews 11:1).

Hearing God's Word repeated out loud will increase our faith to believe God for the impossible. If people do not believe what they read or hear in God's Word, then they are not walking in faith. They are walking in unbelief. Also, if people do not do what they read or hear in God's Word, they are walking in disobedience. If they do not see spiritual breakthrough in many areas of their lives, they could have a lack of faith.

People who struggle with their faith in specific areas should read and meditate on those specific subjects in the Bible until their faith increases. God is looking for breakthrough believers who possess unshakable faith (see Luke 18:8). The unshakable faith of the centurion solider who understood the power of the words and decrees of healing spoken by Jesus is an example to us.

Jesus was not impressed that the soldier had authority, but He was impressed with the soldier's ability to understand the power behind the words spoken by someone in authority. Jesus recognized and was amazed by this kind of great faith. He said that it was a faith that was not found in others in Israel (see Matthew 8:5–13). A person's faith can cause him or her to do the impossible. The centurion soldier's act of faith that drove him to seek out Jesus—the Word—made a way for his paralyzed servant to receive a healing breakthrough.

In other words, desperate times called for this Roman solider to activate the faith required for desperate measures. The breakthrough that you may be in search of may be found in your ability to understand what faith looks like in desperate circumstances. The anatomy of a breakthrough includes your ability to walk by faith and not by what you see in the natural (see 2 Corinthians 5:7).

Faith becomes the anchor for all believers in Christ (see Romans 5:1; Galatians 2:16). The Bible says without faith it is impossible to please the Father (see Hebrews 11:6). Faith and obedience must be embraced for us to gain access to God's breakthrough blessing, favor, provision, healing, deliverance and prosperity. It takes another level of faith to believe and take God at His Word. A person will not have faith in something if they do not believe in what it can accomplish. Faith brings anticipated breakthroughs when truth is the foundation.

Faith is not just in the words we speak, but it is also in the steps we take. Faith is the central theme throughout the Word of God. Things are aligned and realigned in our lives when we change our perspective on life and see it from God's perspective that He communicates in His Word. "Let this mind be in you, which was also in Christ Jesus" (Philippians

2:5 KJV). In this verse, Paul is not encouraging the Church to have Christ's intellect. He is admonishing them to have Christ's attitude toward the Lord's divine will and toward others. When believers possess the mind of Christ through His Word, they will empty and humble themselves as Jesus did. He could have demanded everyone serve Him, but He decided to make Himself of no reputation.

We must follow that same mindset. As co-heirs of Christ and God's children, we should not only speak words of faith in obedience to God's Word, but we should submit fully to His will in order to experience supernatural, unusual breakthrough and favor from the Lord. God does not want us to speak words that are not a part of His biblical and spiritual vocabulary. He wants us to learn His love language through faith (see Hebrews 11:6). We can speak mountain-moving faith that brings breakthrough results. Mark highlights faith and its impact:

> In the morning, as they went along, they saw the fig tree withered from the roots. Peter remembered and said to Jesus, "Rabbi, look! The fig tree you cursed has withered!"
>
> "Have faith in God," Jesus answered. "Truly I tell you, if anyone says to this mountain, 'Go, throw yourself into the sea,' and does not doubt in their heart but believes that what they say will happen, it will be done for them. Therefore I tell you, whatever you ask for in prayer, believe that you have received it, and it will be yours."
>
> Mark 11:20–24

We are to have faith in God. Jesus reveals to His disciples the spiritual principle of a breakthrough. Breakthrough involves seeing the unmovable become movable by speaking out what you believe. Mark instructs his readers that this principle can be applied through prayer when they come before the Father for breakthrough in any area. Faith is the antidote against fear, doubt, unbelief, instability, anxiety and indecisiveness. Faith is the trigger and foundation that releases unusual measures of breakthrough. "For in the gospel the righteousness of God is revealed—a righteousness that is by faith from first to last, just as it is written: 'The righteous will live by faith'" (Romans 1:17).

Hearing Faith

We can see that we are to live in a realm of faith in order for the righteousness of God to be disclosed. Romans 4:16 goes on to say:

> Therefore, the promise comes by faith, so that it may be by grace and may be guaranteed to all Abraham's offspring—not only to those who are of the law but also to those who have the faith of Abraham. He is the father of us all.

Faith is important to possess, as it gives believers access to experience the promises of God that began with Abraham. Our faith only increases when we lean in to hear the Father's voice through the Holy Spirit in prayer and as we learn His Word.

Perhaps at times your faith has been tested; however, trusting, aligning and agreeing with God's Word will release unexpected blessings in unexpected ways from the Lord. What is faith? It is basically taking God at His Word and believing that He exists. Our faith is in God, but we do not properly know the God we should believe in or know how to believe in Him unless He tells us in His Word.

This is why Paul says, "Consequently, faith comes from hearing the message, and the message is heard through the word about Christ" (Romans 10:17). The measure of breakthroughs and the specific call of God on your life will be determined by the measure of faith you obtain from God (see Romans 12:3–8). God has given to each a "measure of faith" to use for Him. This faith is the gift from which all the other gifts flow. Faith is the first gift we receive (for justification), and faith is the gift that brings the other gifts of the Spirit into our lives. When a person is born again, God gives him gifts as a new member of the family of God.

We receive the gifts according to the measure that God has given us, and we exercise the gifts according to the same measure of faith. "To each one of us grace has been given as Christ apportioned it" (Ephesians 4:7). God deals to everyone his portion. Not one single individual receives all the gifts, nor is the same gift distributed to everyone in the same measure. Our sovereign God distributes each gift graciously according to the measure of faith that He has placed upon us.

There are spiritual benefits in obeying God's commands or will.

> "Be strong and very courageous. Be careful to obey all the law my servant Moses gave you; do not turn from it to the right or to the left, that you may be successful wherever you go. Keep this Book of the Law always on your lips; meditate on it day and night, so that you may be careful to do everything written in it. Then you will be prosperous and successful."
>
> Joshua 1:7–8

We can see that prosperity and success were connected to obeying God's ordinances. We are to keep them on our lips and heart constantly. These are God's divine promises that are still available to us today. The Father has benefits that are ready to be released when His children do their part.

I love what Psalm 103:2 says: "Praise the LORD, my soul, and forget not all his benefits." There are benefits that come to those who partner with the Lord Jesus. The Father blesses them with every spiritual blessing in the heavenly realm in Christ (see Ephesians 1:3). There is no other method, template or alternative outside of God's will to receive your spiritual breakthrough—unless you bargain with the devil for worldly possession, power and influence.

Words of Breakthrough Power

In the Word of God there are many promises and instructions on encountering the Father and experiencing the spiritual breakthrough you seek. Getting the breakthrough you are in search of does not come easy when there is an unseen enemy lurking behind the scenes hindering it. In order for God's people to experience breakthrough in their spiritual walk, they must first know what breakthrough looks like.

King David describes his victorious win over the Philistine army like a tsunami that washes away everything in its way. He renames what was once called the Valley of Rephaim (place of giants) to Baal-Perazim (the God who broke out and through). The Lord breached the enemy's frontlines and powerless strongholds that were supported by the baals (false gods) of the Philistines. The Lord proved to be even stronger and more powerful! God wants to give you a breakthrough in those areas of your life in which the enemy appears to be the strongest.

When the Lord of your breakthrough is for you, then who can be against you (see Romans 8:31)? He advances over and above the enemy's floods in your life. God pushes back the enemy's flood of sickness, disease, poverty, fear, depression, lack and all negativity with the flood of His divine blessing, love, favor, joy, peace, righteousness, goodness, healing and every good thing you need in life. The breakthrough is in your words. *Agree*, *align* and *announce* by faith what God has declared that you can possess in His will.

Before we move on to the next chapter, I want to share three components to a breakthrough that I have applied throughout my walk with God. I use them as a template in prayer daily. These three fundamental things that every believer should consider when they pray are:

1. **Agree:** The Bible says, "Again I say to you, if two of you agree on earth about anything they ask, it will be done for them by my Father in heaven" (Matthew 18:19 ESV). Amos 3:3 says, "Do two walk together unless they have agreed to do so?" In other words, walking with the Lord means you are in total agreement with Him and His ways. We are to come into total agreement with God's Word. Even if we happen to disagree with it, God's Word does not change. But His Word has the transformative power to change us. The word *agree* (*agreement*) is the Greek word *sumphoneo*, which means "to be of the same mind, to be harmonious, to agree with one in making a bargain, to come to a mutual understanding."[4]

2. **Align:** According to the *Oxford Dictionary*, the word *align* means "an arrangement in a straight line, or in correct or appropriate relative positions, or a position of agreement or alliance."[5] In other words, it means to set things in a line. Romans 12:2 says, "Do

not conform to the pattern of this world, but be transformed by the renewing of your mind. Then you will be able to test and approve what God's will is—his good, pleasing and perfect will." God wants us to align our will to His. This process must begin with the renewing of our mind through the Word of God. While our minds are spiritual, our brains are physical; therefore, our brains look for homeostasis.

According to *Biology Dictionary*, *homeostasis* is "an organism's process of maintaining a stable internal environment suitable for sustaining life." The word *homeostasis* has Greek roots, with *home*, which means "similar," and *stasis*, which means "stable."[6]

That is why the Bible says, "If any of you lack wisdom, let him ask of God, that giveth to all men liberally, and upbraideth not; and it shall be given him. But let him ask in faith, nothing wavering. For he that wavereth is like a wave of the sea driven with the wind and tossed. For let not that man think that he shall receive any thing of the Lord. A double minded man is unstable in all his ways" (James 1:5–8 KJV).

Stability only comes through a disciplined life in God's Word and in His presence through prayer. We need the proper alignment that only comes by God's Word, and we need to apply it to our spiritual walk as believers.

If God sends you a word that challenges you to grow, your brain is going to fight you every step of the way. Anybody that has been on a diet can testify to the brain's resistance to change. This is why breaking a habit is so challenging! You cannot just break a habit by stopping something—you have to break a habit by creating a new habit. This works by the law of displacement and the law of replacement. If you displace something, you must replace it with something else.

God wants to reset and recalibrate our understanding to be parallel to His. We must align our thoughts to God's divine purpose. "For as he thinketh in his heart, so is he" (Proverbs 23:7 KJV). When we align our thoughts to the Word of God, He straightens out things that are misaligned. Our walk must be upright before the Lord. Walking in obedience to God's Word and doing His will is the proper alignment. Walking with God is a way of life, and it is a choice. We can walk in God's ways or the ways of the world, but we cannot do both (see 2 Kings 8:27; Ephesians 2:2; Matthew 6:24; James 4:4).

3. **Announce by faith:** The word *announce* means "to make known publicly, to give notice of the arrival, presence, or readiness of something, indicate beforehand or to serve as an announcer of."[7] It is imperative that we announce Bible verses by faith. When I do not have the right language or vocabulary, I just announce or speak boldly the Word of God. The more I speak Bible passages, the more my faith increases to receive them. The enemy wants us to stay silent, but the Lord wants us to speak out with confidence. Jesus spoke to the fruitless fig tree and said, "May no one ever eat fruit from you again" (Mark 11:14). Sure enough, what He said happened. The fig tree withered and died. God desires for us to announce His promises daily over our lives by faith until we align and agree with them and until they manifest.

4

Dealing with Hindrances to Breakthrough

And it will be said: "Build up, build up, prepare the road! Remove the obstacles out of the way of my people."

Isaiah 57:14

One of the most challenging things that we will continue to face throughout our Christian walk is dealing with cycles and seasons of resistance, opposition, persecution, temptation and unseen obstacles. It seems that when we are close to the finish line, life trips us up by creating stumbling blocks.

It is the plan of the evil one to disqualify those who are called to run and finish their spiritual race with endurance and momentum (see Hebrews 12:1). The Lord wants His people to pay attention when they are gaining spiritual traction and growing in their faith in Him. The devil looks for opportune times such as those to break their stride.

Types of Resistance

There are types of resistance that come in unexpected ways when we are living life on purpose. These types of oppositions or hindrances that we face commonly include health scares, betrayal, toxic relationships, bad sleeping patterns, unhealthy eating habits, inconsistent dieting and financial hardships. These natural challenges seem as if they are overwhelming and too hard to overcome. We also struggle with emotional and physical challenges such as depression, stress, oppression, anxiety, paranoia, lust, ungodly thoughts and desires, fleshly temptations and appetites, sickness, disease, unexplained illnesses and other bodily difficulties.

Whether it is seen, unseen or supernatural, we must understand that resistance does exist. In one way or another, we will face it. Dealing with resistance from a spiritual and biblical perspective is needed if we are going to have the faith and courage to conquer it. It is not a coincidence that when we are accomplishing the Father's will and purpose, we go through sudden trials, resistance, persecution, opposition and life challenges. You must, however, remain faithful to the Lord in spite of what is working against you in the unseen. You must not choose your will over God's will.

There is no doubt that tough times will come. The first-century believers experienced them, and those living in the last days will as well. Terrible days, however, often come to build believers' character and faith in God. When you go through difficult life circumstances and situations, you must take and leave your burdens at the feet of the Lord (see Psalm 55:22). He will sustain you and help you to break through any unseen barriers and obstacles that are out of your control.

The Bible says, "You make known to me the path of life; in your presence there is fullness of joy; at your right hand are pleasures forevermore" (Psalm 16:11 ESV). In God's presence there is joy, and He will reveal to you the path that leads to life and success. The enemy knows this, and he will do anything in his power to make it difficult for you to achieve your life's goal and spiritual success.

Lord of the Breakthrough

The Lord wants to bless those who are His and bring them into a place called breakthrough. He is the Lord of the breakthrough, and He will fight for you when breakthrough seems unreachable. If He is called the Lord of the Breaker (see Micah 2:13 AMP), the Breach (see 2 Samuel 5:20 AMP, CEV) and the Breakthrough, then He is the War General in battle that can accomplish that for you.

David could not do it alone (see 1 Chronicles 14:8–17; 2 Samuel 5:17–25). He could only achieve breakthrough with the supernatural help and counsel of the Lord in the battle. How many spiritual battles and victories have we missed because we did not take the time to seek God on a matter in spiritual warfare resistance?

King David addressed the resistance to his breakthrough by inquiring of the Lord. The Lord gave him a strategy against the Philistine army that ultimately facilitated a breakthrough that was like a gushing river. David made this statement of what God did for him in two different battles against his enemy: "The LORD has broken through my enemies before me like the breakthrough of waters" (2 Samuel 5:20 NASB). We should seek the Lord first to find out exactly what we are up against and how we should conquer those places, people and things that are blocking us.

Every resistance or setback is not created by the enemy, but things such as wrong relationships and alignments can hinder us. Also, certain geographical locations can be environments of hindrance if they are not conducive for expansion, growth or success. Even places of employment or places of worship can work against us if the Lord is requiring us to go in a new direction. There are many factors to consider when it comes to natural and spiritual hindrances.

Believers often overspiritualize hindrances by blaming every setback on the enemy. But could it be that we become our biggest hindrance by assisting the enemy when we disobey the Father's instructions and wisdom for our lives? It is easier to blame-shift than to take full responsibility over our spiritual growth and decisions.

It is wise to ask the Father what specific, unseen things are delaying your breakthrough. Do not allow the enemy to dupe you into believing that God does not want you to experience His blessings. They only can happen, however, through the act of obedience.

Discern the Hindrance

Anything that is restraining or restricting you from prayer, fasting, reading and studying the Word of God, spending time with the Father or going to the next level in your relationship and communion with the Holy Spirit will require spiritual breakthrough. Believers must be able to locate and discern where they are experiencing their greatest setbacks or resistance. They must then determine what necessary steps and plans of action are required to receive breakthrough in those areas.

Do not take matters in your own hands. Seek the wisdom and timing of God. Paul and Silas encountered a hindering spirit through a fortune-teller on their way to prayer (see Acts 16:16–18). It took several days for Paul to discern what was the source of her powers. He did not assume that he knew, but he discerned accurately with the help of Holy Spirit. Later, Paul rebuked the spirit in the name of Jesus and commanded it to come out of her. He needed the power and authority in Jesus' name to address this preventing spirit.

Discerning of spirits is needed vitally in the Body of Christ to deal with spiritual backlash, retaliation, setback, opposition, resistance or demonic hindrances. To embrace and encounter spiritual breakthroughs, we must first discern spiritually what invisible hindrances are present. Spiritual discernment is required to recognize and deal with spiritual matters (see 1 Corinthians 2:14). No matter what attacks the enemy decides to send your direction to break you down, you will achieve breakthrough by the power of God through the Holy Spirit in you.

When trials and setbacks come unexpectedly to put a hold on your life, the Bible says to rejoice.

> Consider it pure joy, my brothers, when you encounter trials of many kinds, because you know that the testing of your faith develops perseverance. Allow perseverance to finish its work, so that you may be mature and complete, not lacking anything.
>
> James 1:2–4 BSB

This sounds like a hard thing to do when subtle or blatant obstacles continue to show up. These hidden agendas and setbacks that force delays can cause us to lose all hope and confidence. We must understand that God will provide His power to overcome all that comes our way, which is why we can have joy. We often misread what Paul wrote in Corinthians. "No temptation has overtaken you except what is common to mankind. And God is faithful; he will not let you be tempted beyond what you can bear" (1 Corinthians 10:13).

This verse, spoken by Paul, means that the strength of the temptations that believers face will be proportionate to the strength that God gives His people to resist them. We often misinterpret this verse to mean that the Father will not permit unfortunate things to occur in our lives that we cannot bear. Such an interpretation contradicts Paul's later writings, where he goes into detail about the hardship and great pressure he encountered in Asia. These hardships were far beyond his ability to endure, to the point that he despaired of hope and life itself (see 2 Corinthians 1:8–9). God will allow us to experience difficulties in life that are too much for us to bear so that we can learn to depend on His supernatural strength and not rely solely on our own strength (see 2 Corinthians 1:10).

He knows what worldly temptations or works of the enemy we are able to overcome by the help of the Holy Spirit. God never said that we would not have problems. We should arm ourselves with God's Word by humbling and submitting ourselves to it and to God. If we do that, we can resist the devil and he will flee.

Hindered Prayer

We are to deal with spiritual matters before they become spiritual snares that are used of the enemy. "'In your anger do not sin': Do not let the sun go down while you are still angry, and do not give the devil a foothold" (Ephesians 4:26–27). When I am not seeing breakthroughs in my life, I do a spiritual audit—an assessment and inventory—of any possible unresolved issues, unrepented or unconfessed sins, unforgiveness, anger, strife or bitterness in my heart toward others. Those types of things become stumbling blocks.

Did you know that we can become a stumbling block for others? We can hinder their breakthrough, salvation or the fulfillment of God's calling (see 1 Corinthians 10:32–33). We must recognize how we could become stumbling blocks for others, and we must recognize the stumbling blocks that others can create for us. Prayer becomes the central place where breakthrough happens for believers.

Daniel's breakthrough was held up in the unseen for 21 days (see Daniel 10). There were ruling principalities (princes of Persia and Greece) blocking and prohibiting the answer to his prayer being able to come from heaven to earth. Daniel's prayer was delayed due to satanic influences and powers. The kingdom of darkness (Satan's sphere and domain) is relentlessly fighting against Christ's Church. The Bible reveals that the believer's war is not against flesh and blood (each other), but against principalities, powers, rulers of the darkness of this world and spiritual wickedness in high places (see Ephesians 6:12).

Technically, God did not instruct Daniel to go on a 21-day fast for a breakthrough. He had already been praying relentlessly for 21 days until his breakthrough revelation and answer came. On day 21 of his fast, the archangel, Gabriel, explained to him why his prayer's answer had been hindered. Daniel's response in dealing with unseen opposition to his breakthrough was that he never ceased from praying (see Daniel 10:11–13).

His consistent and persistent prayers caused the Lord to send Gabriel and the archangel Michael, a warring general angel, to bring breakthrough for Daniel. He already lived a life of prayer and fasting (see Daniel 1:8–16). He shows us that prayer and fasting, coupled with persistent faith, can create a space for our breakthrough to come through.

The Word of God contains a plethora of stories about ordinary people who were able to accomplish amazing feats while overcoming and breaking through in times of crisis. It is a spiritual handbook and encyclopedia with many subjects, examples, stories and outcomes that will assist every believer as they try to address spiritual and natural hindrances to receiving God's breakthroughs. The Bible's primary theme, from Genesis to Revelation, is breakthrough.

What do you do when you have swung with all your might trying to hit the ball, but the devil has thrown you an unexpected curve ball? You must put on the whole armor of God to stand against any purposely thrown obstacles sent by the enemy (see Ephesians 6:11–24). When you get hit or knocked down, you must make the decision to rise to the occasion, even when all odds are stacked against you.

You can do all things through Christ who strengthens you (see Philippians 4:13), and you are more than a conqueror (see Romans 8:37), who can overcome any spiritual resistance (see 1 John 4:4). The victory is yours by faith, not by your works. When the enemy comes to make life slippery enough that you fall, God will become your shield of salvation and help so that you will not lose your footing (see Psalm 18:35–37).

God's Restraining Order

Regardless of what you have accomplished or how you may have failed or fallen in the past, you are an overcomer by the blood of the Lamb (see Romans 8:31–39). Stand in your authority and do not lose sight of God's promises for you. The power of breaking through strongholds, obstacles or the challenges of life is to allow God to fight your battles (see 2 Chronicles 20:15). I love what the prophet Isaiah declares: "When the enemy shall come in like a flood, the Spirit of the LORD shall lift up a standard against him" (Isaiah 59:19 KJV).

It is the Spirit of the Lord who will lift up a heavenly standard for you against the evil one. What will the Lord lift up? He will lift up His Law, decree, will and word of protection. God will place a restraining order against the enemy as He did when Satan wanted to touch Job. The Lord permitted Satan to afflict Job's body, and yet He restrained him from taking Job's life (see Job 2:3–6).

In Job's life, we can see the Lord's restraining power demonstrated three times. First, He restrained the devil from doing whatever he wanted. Second, He allowed Satan to afflict Job in every way possible except taking his life. Third, the Lord permitted the enemy to confiscate Job's wealth and assets. In spite of what Job endured, he never gave up or cursed God—even when his own wife encouraged him to do so (see Job 2:9). As a result, he received double restitution of blessing from the Lord. His breakthrough blessing came as he prayed for others, and God granted him double for his trouble (see Job 42:10).

Sin and disobedience prevent spiritual breakthrough in the believer's life. The word *sin*, as it appears in Scripture, comes from the Greek word *hamartia*, or the Hebrew word *hata*. They both mean "to miss the mark . . . to err, be mistaken . . . to miss or wander from the path of uprightness . . . to be without a share in . . . [to] violate God's law."[1] The word *hata* was used in spear and ax throwing and archery. When a person sins, he or she is missing the center of his or her target. This is an important question to ask yourself: What target in your life have you missed or failed to hit accurately?

Job did not sin against God when his wealth, health and faith were tested. Some people only trust God when things in life are going normally. Will you remain faithful to the Lord when everything is not going so well? There are those who put their trust in material things, but there are others who put their trust solely in the Lord (see Psalm 20:7).

Job was under protective custody in God's care. When God told Satan not to touch Job's life, He placed a restraining decree on him. There is sanctuary at the altar of prayer when you are part of the Body of Christ. When the devil is trying to stop you dead in your tracks, remember that "the steps of a good man are ordered by the LORD: and he delighteth in his way" (Psalm 37:23 KJV). It is the plan of the enemy to get you off course, but the Holy Spirit will direct your steps toward freedom and fulfillment.

In this Christian walk, you will be met with sudden disappointments, mishaps, misfortune, surprises and temptation. They will come to attack you mentally, physically, financially, naturally, emotionally and spiritually. We must, however, stand on what God's Word of truth says. "Resist the devil [by firm reliance upon the Lord], and he will flee from you" (James 4:7). Trouble is no respecter of persons, as Job found out. He also, however, found safety in prayer. In the Bible, people are no strangers to life's trials and tribulations. They handle hindrances with help from the Lord.

Overcoming the Opposition

Jesus is the epitome of someone who overcame Satan, sin, death, hell and the grave. He ascended in victory and sits at the right hand of the Father (see Hebrews 1:3; 12:2; 1 Peter 3:22). You do not have to succumb or fall prey to demonic hindrances that are set up against you. God has an excellent history of making a way of escape for those who seek and trust Him in faith. John tells us, "For everyone born of God overcomes the world. This is the victory that has overcome the world, even our faith" (1 John 5:4).

He wants His disciples to know that those who are born of God have the supernatural power to overcome and break through life's challenges and temptations. We must have peace in the midst of the storm. What you may be facing currently is not permanent. Storms will pass when we learn how to weather them. "These things I have spoken unto you, that in me ye might have peace. In the world ye shall have tribulation: but be of good cheer; I have overcome the world" (John 16:33 KJV).

Since Jesus overcame the world, we, too, can overcome by God's power through the Holy Spirit. There is a blessing that comes to those who can overcome the worldly temptations with which the enemy entices believers. It is the devil's ploy to draw us back into our old sin nature. He wants to seduce and deceive us into believing that where we came from is better than where we are presently. James confirms that, "Blessed is the man that endureth temptation: for when he is tried, he shall receive the crown of life, which the Lord hath promised to them that love him" (James 1:12 KJV).

There are saints who have passed on that are cheering for you daily to overcome your personal challenges with sin. It will take spiritual maturation and the strength of the Holy Spirit to break through those tempting barriers.

> Wherefore seeing we also are compassed about with so great a cloud of witnesses, let us lay aside every weight, and the sin which doth so easily beset us, and let us run with patience the race that is set before us, looking unto Jesus the author and finisher of our faith; who for the joy that was set before him endured the cross, despising the shame, and is set down at the right hand of the throne of God.
>
> Hebrews 12:1–2 KJV

The above text says that we are to lay aside every weight and sin that comes to hinder us. The apostle Paul understood this principle as he fulfilled his ministry. He said, "I press toward the mark for the prize of the high calling of God in Christ Jesus" (Philippians 3:14 KJV). His daily mission was not to miss the mark (to sin); his mission was to fulfill his calling in God. Paul understood the vigorous training and discipline that is required to be a follower of Christ. He compared it to an athlete who competes for a prize or award.

> Everyone who competes in the games trains with strict discipline. They do it for a crown that is perishable, but we do it for a crown that is imperishable. Therefore I do not run aimlessly; I do not fight like I am beating the air. No, I discipline my body and make it my slave, so that after I have preached to others, I myself will not be disqualified.
>
> 1 Corinthians 9:25–27 BSB

Prophetic Warfare

Paul encourages, charges and commends his spiritual son, Timothy, to use prophecy as a weapon of war against falsehood, heresy, division, temptation and anything that would hinder his advancement as a leader in the Church.

> This command I entrust to you, Timothy, my son, in accordance with the prophecies previously made concerning you, that by them you fight the good fight, keeping faith and a good conscience, which some have rejected and suffered shipwreck in regard to their faith.
>
> 1 Timothy 1:18–19 NASB1995

He admonishes Timothy to wage prophetic warfare with the prophecies he received from the Lord. This unseen warfare is not of his own doing. It is a war that has been instigated and initiated by the devil. Timothy is encouraged to use the Word of the Lord as a weapon that he is to wield in the spiritual war. He was to fight with the prophetic word.

God's promises that are spoken over our lives are what the adversary hates, and he is trying to put up resistance against those who are called of God in faith. The way to win this invisible battle is to use spiritual weapons of warfare (see 2 Corinthians 10:4–7). We are on the winning side. "If God is for us, who can be against us?" (Romans 8:31).

The Lord will not have us be ignorant of the devil's schemes or trickery. Fight back with the promises in God's Word. The Bible says that the promises of the Lord are yes and amen (see 2 Corinthians 1:20). They are ours as our inheritance. Breakthrough is our inheritance as believers in Christ. Even Timothy was instructed and encouraged by the apostle Paul to keep the faith, be sober minded and have a good conscience.

Others have rejected these instructions, and they suffered shipwreck as they were unprepared when times of testing came. You must keep in mind that when God's promises and prophetic words are released over you, the enemy does not have previous knowledge or intel about them. When they are spoken, he catches wind and sends his demonic cohorts and assailants to try to fight your prophetic word of the Lord, dream, vision or God's promises.

The greater the resistance that the devil puts up against you, the greater the promises and breakthrough you can expect. It is good to know that every difficulty, setback, delay, resistance or unexpected hindrance to you receiving your breakthrough is not in vain. It is only an indication that your breakthrough is on the way. When Jesus was called to the cross to die for the penalty of sin in the world, His own disciple, Peter, was influenced by Satan and became a hindrance to the purposes of the Father.

Jesus was able to discern quickly who was speaking through Peter, and He rebuked Satan. Interestingly enough, as Jesus rebuked Peter, He used the same words that He used to rebuke the devil in his temptation in the wilderness (see Matthew 4:10). Peter was acting the enemy's part by opposing the will of God as an offense (stumbling block).

Do Not Get Duped by the Enemy

Jesus always seemed to put Satan in his rightful place as a liar, deceiver and accuser by fighting back with truth. In order to overcome the enemy and the spiritual booby traps that he sets up throughout your walk with Christ, you are to arm yourselves with truth in God's Word. A booby trap is a device or setup that is intended to kill, harm or surprise a person or animal. The nature of the enemy is to kill, steal and destroy both you and God's purposes in your life (see John 10:10). When you align your faith and your words with God's will, you hinder Satan's agenda.

We are to win souls for Christ and fulfill our earthly ministry duties as sons of God (see Colossians 4:17). I have come to notice that the enemy is looking for weaklings—faithless, fearful, ignorant and feeble-minded people whom he can devour like prey. He is described in the Bible as a roaring lion or a charging bear (see 1 Peter 5:8; Proverbs 28:15). Even in the natural, you are never to turn your back on a predator. Losing your focus becomes an opportunity for them to pounce on you. You must stand your ground, look the enemy in the eyes and declare God's Word that you will not be moved (see Psalm 112:6; Proverbs 10:30).

We can stand upon the truth of Psalm 27:2 (NLT), which says, "When evil people come to devour me, when my enemies and foes attack me, they will stumble and fall."

Discerning Demonic or Godly Delays

There are demonic delays set up by the devil; however, there are also divine delays established by God. We must understand and discern the difference between the two. Demonic delays are created so that God's people will miss divine seasons of breakthrough, blessings, favor and major opportunities. They are created to derail, offset, resist and block the promises and blessings of God. They are designed to lead believers to walk in disobedience and go around in circles like a dog chasing its tail. They are also purposed to wear out the saint and have them believe that God's promises will never be obtained. A satanic delay, in other words, is when an individual gets stuck aimlessly in one spot.

Demonic delays become a tireless cycle in which people find it difficult to excel or to have momentum. They cause people to feel as if they are a guinea pig that is running in place on a stationary wheel. A demonic delay is meant to bind and restrict a person so that they will not be able to fulfill their destiny. Moreover, spiritual struggles, hardships and sorrow are signs and results of demonic delays and hindrances. Satanic delays and denials cause a person extreme discontentment and frustrations. When people's blessings are prevented from manifesting despite so much effort and labor, they often question God or lose their faith.

On the other hand, there are divine delays sent by God. These are to protect, teach and instill wisdom to His people. God brings delays to teach us humility, obedience and perseverance. There are those who cannot determine a divine delay from a demonic one, and that causes them to fight against God's preventive and protective tactics. They feel that every delay comes from the devil and not from God.

Every decision we make must be backed by the Word of God and the direction of the Holy Spirit. We have to lean into what God is saying so that we will not make life mistakes or find ourselves in recurring cycles of delay and resistance. I often remind people that everything is not the devil, but our decisions can create unnecessary problems, resistance or hindrances. Our actions must align with God's will in faith. In obedience, we must trust that He will lead us to a path of success and truth. The Bible asks a profound question in Galatians 5:7: "You were running a good race. Who cut in on you to keep you from obeying the truth?"

Breaking Curses

There are word curses and generational curses. Both are unseen hindrances for people. The definition of the word *curse* is "a prayer or invocation for harm or injury to come upon one, and a profane or obscene oath or word."[2] There is power in both word curses and generational curses. They can bring injury, harm and pain. A generational curse is believed to be passed down from one generation to another due to rebellion against the Lord.

If your family line is plagued by poverty, anger, divorce, incest or other ungodly patterns, you are likely under a generational curse (see Exodus 20:5; 34:7; Numbers 14:18; Deuteronomy 5:9). The cure for a generational curse has always been repentance. When Israel turned from idols to worshiping the Lord, the curse was suddenly broken. He saved and rescued them (see Judges 3:9, 15; 1 Samuel 12:10–11).

A word curse is the opposite of a spoken blessing. It is a spoken or verbalized word that is declared over an individual's life, and it brings injury, harm or destruction. Unfortunately, word curses possess tremendous power when they come from those in seats of authority such as parents, teachers, mentors, coaches and spiritual leaders. Oftentimes, these word curses are not spoken intentionally. The one cursing is unaware that he or she is putting a curse on someone. People just do not realize the potency that their words carry.

When a parent, for example, says to a child, "You are so stupid. You will never amount to anything," that parent is cursing their child. The word curse will not take full effect automatically unless the child receives and believes those words spoken. If he or she does, however, those words will be lodged into his or her soul and have a negative impact on the child's mind, will and emotions. Over time, those words will become a force for harm. It is not uncommon for demonic spirits to attach themselves to word curses. When that happens, the lies that were spoken are reinforced and empowered.

Individuals who are worried about a curse, either a generational or a word curse, can find the answer in salvation through Jesus Christ. Scripture says that these curses are in connection to our choices (see Deuteronomy 30:19–20), and they can be broken by knowledge of God's Word. We must realize that we have the authority to break them. Safeguard yourself from sin and anything that would lure you away from fulfilling God's purpose and will. Curses are real and should never be overlooked or underestimated.

5

Unlocking Daily Revelation
for Supernatural Breakthrough

I waited patiently for the LORD; he turned to me and heard my cry. He lifted me out of the slimy pit, out of the mud and mire; he set my feet on a rock and gave me a firm place to stand.

Psalm 40:1–2

The Father wants His people to seek Him daily for fresh revelation. He wants us to cooperate with the Holy Spirit to see heaven's purposes manifested in our lives. We have been given access to go boldly before the throne of grace in prayer so that we will obtain mercy and find grace to assist us in times of need (see Hebrews 4:16). It is because of the Lord's great love that we are not consumed, for His compassion toward us never fails.

As we seek Him daily for insight, wisdom, understanding and direction, the Bible says that His mercy and His faithfulness are fresh each morning (see Lamentations 3:23). He unlocks daily revelation about how we are to walk in wisdom and shun evil. "And unto man he said, Behold, the fear of the Lord, that is wisdom; and to depart from evil is understanding" (Job 28:28 KJV).

It is in the place of prayer that God gives us answers to life's problems. Prayer helps us handle the invisible resistance to healing, deliverance, restoration, blessings and breakthrough that we face, and God will expose the wicked plans of the enemy (see Job 27:7–17). We often expect God to remove problems, but He wants to give us a plan of action to solve the problems. God did not remove the Red Sea for Moses and the children of Israel. He parted it. When the Lord does not remove our problems, He always makes a way through them for us.

Blessed, but Not Broken

We may find ourselves having to make life-altering decisions while at the same time feeling broken. We know what God has said about us in His Word, but at times we feel perplexed, bruised, rejected, abandoned, hurt, confused or isolated from others. We wrestle with our identity and calling in God and try to do our best to fulfill His will for our life.

Jacob found himself running from his angry brother, Esau (see Genesis 32). It was in this state that he encountered God in the wilderness. The Lord wanted him to face his own fears and not run from his responsibilities. Regardless of how Jacob may have felt as he ran for his life, he never lost sight of what God had promised. As he wrestled with the Angel of the Lord, he was crippled. After that, Jacob had to hold on to God's promises while walking with a limp. God said,

"Let me go, for the day breaketh. And he said, I will not let thee go, except thou bless me" (Genesis 32:26 KJV).

Have you wrestled with your calling or your identity? Have you wrestled with a dream, vision, prophetic word or promise? What are those life hindrances and challenges that are keeping you from pursuing the Lord's promises? The Father wants to unlock a treasure chest of revelation for you every day so that you receive His best.

Jacob wrestled with the Lord all night until the day broke. He was determined to get his breakthrough. Jacob knew that his brother, Esau, was after him to take him out. He understood that he had to eventually face him and that he could not fight or run while disabled. He could have easily grown bitter because of what was happening to him, but he did not.

When God told him, "Let Me go, for the dawn is breaking," Jacob clung to the Lord with all of his might, even while crippled. He gave this unexpected response: "I will not let You go unless You bless me." The enemy wants us to zoom in and focus solely on every invisible hindrance, setback, obstacle, challenge, persecution, resistance, sickness, disease, pain or suffering so that he can break us down and break our will. But God wants us to hold on to His promises and never let go of what He has said over us. We should not get distracted or blindsided by the enemy. We can expect a breakthrough from the Lord daily by faith if we believe and fight for it through His Word.

We know that Jacob was not a match to an all-powerful God. Even still, his heart that was unyielding, unwavering and unflinching caused him to experience a blessing. In this wrestling match that we call life, what are you willing to fight for? What are you willing to give up to receive your daily breakthrough blessing from the Father? If you contend in prayer for your breakthrough and are obedient to His Word, He will give you what you deserve.

Hearing God's Voice Brings Breakthrough

Hearing the voice of God is important if you want to experience breakthrough on a continual basis. Hearing and recognizing the voice of the Father, as opposed to your own voice or the voice of the enemy, will allow you to excel in your spiritual growth. So often, we lean into our own desires and mix them with God's will assuming that He will approve of them. God's voice, counsel and thoughts on a situation matter. Our thoughts and ways are nothing like the way God thinks (see Isaiah 55:8–9). With the Holy Spirit's help, we must align our thoughts and ways to the Father's thoughts and ways. This process can only be accomplished by reading and knowing His Word.

In addition, believers should be able to discern which voice is more influential. We should be able to know the difference between:

- God's voice (Spirit of His Word)
- Human spirit (your own voice)
- Demonic spirits (deceptive, seducing and luring influences)

As children of God, it is essential to our spiritual growth that we are able to discern the voice of the Father in our life. We do not want to be led astray or deceived by an unfamiliar voice or strange influence (see John 10:27). We serve a living God, who is always speaking to us through creation, through

His Holy Bible and through His Spirit. Hearing the voice of the Father requires knowing who is speaking to us. We must learn how to hear and listen to God's voice. Hearing and listening are two different things.

When we recognize that it is the Lord who is speaking to us, we must learn to listen to His instructions and obey them (see Proverbs 19:20; Psalm 32:8; 2 Timothy 3:16–17). Having an ear that listens to the voice of God daily will cause us to make right decisions that will bring about breakthrough, healing, deliverance, protection, direction and provision to fulfill our calling in the earth.

We must learn to discern God's voice and His will through His Word. To know His will is to learn His Word and to walk in His ways. Discerning the voice of the enemy is easy when what he says does not line up with Word of God. When my spirit is unsettled, I am able to dismiss any contrary voice of the enemy that is speaking to my mind. To experience daily advances, progress and breakthroughs from the Father, we must be open and available to hear His instructions.

> The Lord GOD has given Me the tongue of disciples, so that I may know how to sustain the weary one with a word. He awakens Me morning by morning, He awakens My ear to listen as a disciple. The Lord GOD has opened My ear, and I was not disobedient, nor did I turn back.
>
> Isaiah 50:4–5 NASB

The above passage assures us that the Father will disciple and teach those who seek Him. In addition, the Lord is looking for those who will give their lives totally over to Him. That is why the Gospel being preached is important. It gives individuals who are lost a chance to hear and respond accordingly. He is in search of listening hearts—not hardened ones. The Baptist pastor who led me to give my life over to Jesus often quoted the following passage:

> So, as the Holy Spirit says: "Today, if you hear his voice, do not harden your hearts as you did in the rebellion, during the time of testing in the wilderness, where your ancestors tested and tried me, though for forty years they saw what I did. That is why I was angry with that generation; I said, 'Their hearts are always going astray, and they have not known my ways.' So I declared on oath in my anger, 'They shall never enter my rest.'"
>
> Hebrews 3:7–11

What stood out to me in this Scripture passage was the instruction not to harden my heart as those who rebelled in the day of testing did. God will break through every desert place that comes to restrain us. He will come to our rescue in the valley of decision and draw us closer to Him.

Surrendering my life to Jesus was the best decision I ever made, and it made hell nervous. When you make the decision to respond to God's Word daily by listening and obeying His voice in prayer, you make hell shake and give the enemy a nervous breakdown!

Knowing God's Word Brings Breakthrough

Knowing what the Bible teaches is important when you are trying to listen to the voice of the Lord. It is imperative to know the Word of God for yourself, not only for spiritual maturation, but also for standing against the wiles of the devil in times of testing, trials, tribulation and uncertainty (see Ephesians 6:11). Other Bible versions use the words *strategies, evil tricks* and *devilish schemes* rather than the word *wiles*. The word *wiles* means "manipulation or tricks designed to deceive a person."[1]

It is important to understand the Word of God in order to not be outwitted by the enemy's war game of deception, temptation and accusation. When followers of Jesus devote themselves to reading, studying and knowing Scripture for themselves, their faith becomes unshakable. It becomes a fortified wall of defense against the works of the enemy with which he seduces God's people. With their faith, God's people become unmovable in their revelation of who they are in Christ Jesus.

The Lord desires to unleash supernatural faith within every believer. He wants us to experience supernatural breakthrough when we align ourselves with what He has declared, decreed and prophesied. These are three acts of the rules of engagement against the believer that the enemy deploys— deception, temptation and accusation. I believe one of the most cunning strategies that the enemy unleashes against followers of Christ is to hinder their spiritual breakthrough by:

1. Deception (see John 8:44; 2 John 1:7; Matthew 7:15; 1 Timothy 4:1; 2 Corinthians 11:3, 14; Acts 5:3).
2. Temptation (see Matthew 4:1–11; 1 Thessalonians 3:5; 1 John 3:8–10; 1 Corinthians 7:5).
3. Accusation (see Matthew 27:40; 1 Timothy 5:19; Revelation 12:10; Zechariah 3:1).

Understanding these three strategies will help every believer arm themselves accurately when studying and learning the Word of God. It will help them operate in their legal right and authority when dealing with unseen obstacles or demonic resistance. Examples of spiritual hindrances include pride, fear, unbelief, lack of passion, occultism (belief in power such as magic, spiritism, theosophy and alchemy), passivity, lack of knowledge, identity crisis, sin, unforgiveness and curses. Knowing what the Bible has to say concerning theses hindrances will assist us in knowing how to overcome them. Our knowledge will help us defeat the works of the devil with the truth. Knowing the truth will help us fight against deception.

I believe that natural obstacles can block our spiritual development and growth. Knowing the remedy and truth in God's Word will help us avoid and rid ourselves of them. This truth comes by knowing the Lord and Savior who gave Himself for the Church. Jesus disarms all the powers and authorities. He made a public spectacle of them, triumphing over them with the cross (see Colossians 2:15).

Knowing the Word of God draws us even closer to the Father. When we understand God's Word, we can also know His will, which He reveals through believers. "For prophecy never had its origin in the human will, but prophets, though human, spoke from God as they were carried along by the Holy Spirit" (2 Peter 1:21). We can know God's mind, will and eternal purposes. They are defined and revealed through prophetic utterances by prophetic voices. The Holy Spirit brings supernatural revelation of God's will to humans.

Knowing God's Heart Will Bring Breakthrough

Knowing the heart of the Father is as important as knowing His Word, voice and will. God's heart is always connected to His Word. Worship and communion with the Holy Spirit will give us access to His heartstrings. God has emotions and thoughts that He desires to reveal to those who are His.

The heart refers to the central part in an individual's body. The Bible says that the heart is the nature of a person, and to know the heart of an individual is to understand his or her innermost feelings, desires, intentions, thoughts, inclinations or character (see Proverbs 4:23; 16:1). Likewise, the Lord's heart is the essence of who He is, which is His will, purpose, desires and thoughts.

By studying the Word of God, hearing God's voice, spending time in prayer and worship, and knowing Jesus, we will be able to know the heart of the Father. It is through knowing the Bible that God's heart is revealed. To understand the Father's heart and will, we must read, study and meditate on His Word. God reveals the revelation of Himself and His message to all who seek Him.

When a fan studies a celebrity, or they read or watch the celebrity's autobiography or documentary, they get a better idea of who the celebrity or public figure really is. The fan feels a personal connection to the person even though he or she does not know the celebrity personally. Historians read letters or journals and listen to past interviews to get a better understanding of what historical people's lives were like and what their influences and motivations were. God has given His people a profound way to know Him and what happened before man existed through His eternal Word.

By reading God's Word, we draw closer to His heart. We begin to think how He thinks, because the Bible was divinely breathed out by Him (see 2 Timothy 3:16). From the book of Genesis to the book of Revelation, the entire Bible reveals the nature, mind, heart and will of God, while unveiling to us who He is and what He is like.

Simply reading the Bible as you would read any book will not bring you any closer to the heart of God (see John 5:39). The goal of reading God's Word should not be reading to get information, but rather reading to receive a divine impartation of who God is. Reading the Word of God with the help of the Holy Spirit for the purpose of getting to know God's heart should cause you to desire to worship and love Him. The process of studying and reading the Bible also reveals Jesus, who is the Word. Knowing Jesus reveals God's heart. Jesus said that anyone who sees Him has also seen the Father (see John 14:9).

When you gave your life to Jesus, the Father was the one who was drawing you closer to Him by invitation. Your heart responded to the Father's heart. No individual can know God's heart without knowing, trusting and experiencing the power of salvation through the Gospel message of Jesus. Jesus reveals the Father in heaven. "He [Jesus] is the image of the invisible God" (Colossians 1:15 ESV). Since Jesus and the Father are one, Jesus visually signifies God's heart, the essence of who the Father is (see John 10:30).

It is vitally important that we understand that it is through prayer that God reveals His heart to us. Praying in the Spirit is the language in which the Holy Spirit articulates, interprets and translates what God's will is for us each day (see 1 Corinthians 2:10–11; Romans 8:26–28; John 14:26). Spending time with the Father in prayer allows us to assess accurately His heart. A child must spend time with his or her parents to get to know them personally. As children of God, we must spend time with the Lord in prayer to understand Him more intimately, deeply and personally. "Draw near to God, and he will draw near to you. Cleanse your hands, you sinners, and purify your hearts, you double-minded" (James 4:8 ESV).

Obeying God's Word Brings Breakthrough

Spending alone time with the Lord in prayer will create a greater level of intimacy between you and the Father, and it will establish a deeper relationship in which your desires will become more aligned with His.

We must pursue God's heart. He wants to bless us, but we should not pursue only what He can provide us. Pursuing His heart is a serious endeavor, as knowing Him will bring spiritual transformation. The more we lean into learning about the Father, the more connected we will be. And we will begin to long for the Father and declare as the psalmist David did, "As the deer longs for streams of water, so I long for you, O God" (Psalm 42:1 NLT).

Obeying God's Word with the help of the Holy Spirit will remind us of God's will, and it will give us the power and the keys to experience radical blessing, total restoration, freedom, healing, miracles, financial provision and breakthrough. The Lord does not bless those who are disobedient. Disobeying God's heart and the truth that is revealed in the Bible will bring about judgment and divine correction. "So Jesus said to the Jews who had believed him, 'If you abide in my word, you are truly my disciples, and you will know the truth, and the truth will set you free'" (John 8:31–32 ESV). True followers of Christ obey the Word and the will of the Father. The truth will always bring healing, deliverance and breakthrough to those who obey His Word.

> But be doers of the word, and not hearers only, deceiving yourselves. For if anyone is a hearer of the word and not a doer, he is like a man who looks intently at his natural face in a mirror. For he looks at himself and goes away and at once forgets what he was like. But the one who looks into the perfect

law, the law of liberty, and perseveres, being no hearer who forgets but a doer who acts, he will be blessed in his doing.

James 1:22–25 ESV

Being a doer and not just a hearer of the Word blesses those who are obedient. Jesus tells us that those who do not do the will of the Father will not enter the Kingdom of heaven (see Matthew 7:21–23).

Fasting Brings Supernatural Breakthrough

Fasting is one of the most powerful ingredients to receiving divine breakthrough. Do you feel as if something is holding you back? Did you know that fasting can break spiritual strongholds off your life? The Bible says in Isaiah 58:6, "Is not this the kind of fasting I have chosen: to loose the chains of injustice and untie the cords of the yoke, to set the oppressed free and break every yoke?" I have experienced unusual breakthroughs when I have fasted and sought the Lord concerning unseen opposition and setbacks in my life.

There are six types of fasting for spiritual breakthrough. They are tools for growth, healing, deliverance and financial breakthrough. The Lord will direct you as to what type of fast you should take to get the results you need. Below, I have provided which fast in the Bible worked in specific situations. It is always wise to seek medical advice and attention before going on a fast. Here are the various fasts revealed in the Word of God that can unlock revelation for supernatural breakthrough and victory:

- Jesus Christ fasted for an extended period of time (forty days and nights) for spiritual power and victory over temptation, the flesh and the devil (see Matthew 4:1–2).

- John the Baptist and his disciples fasted often to enhance their fellowship with the Lord and to be effective witnesses. If believers fast to help their testimonies have an impact on many for Christ, the Lord will bless them for His glory (see Matthew 9:14; Luke 4:1–2; Mark 2:18).

- Jesus' disciples should fast to draw closer to Him to see total deliverance from sin, bondage, spiritual hindrances, strongholds and addictions. If believers fast, they have the power to break the power of sin and the addictions that come to limit their liberty in Christ (see Matthew 9:15; 17:21; John 3:28–29).

- The apostle Paul fasted to receive divine direction and supernatural physical healing. If believers fast and submit their will to the Father, He will reveal His will to them in prayer (see Acts 9:9).

- The widow woman fasted to provide a meal for a stranger in need. The widow decided to go without food to meet the physical needs of someone else. Due to her sacrifice and faith to obey God through the prophet Elijah's instructions, the Lord made sure that she and her son had more than enough food (see 1 Kings 17:7–16).

- Samuel the prophet fasted for national repentance, revival and restoration. The people were bound by idol worship and needed deliverance. As leader over Israel, Samuel called his people to seek the Lord and to bring the Ark of the Covenant back to Jerusalem. If believers fast and pray, a spiritual awakening and revival will take place, and the Lord will pour out His Spirit on the people (see 1 Samuel 7:6).

- Elijah the prophet fasted for mental freedom from emotional despair, fear of death and anxiety. Through fasting, the Lord will reveal to His people how to overcome emotional problems, destructive habits, fear and other challenges that life brings (see 1 Kings 19:4–8).

- Ezra, the scribe and priest, fasted for the Lord's supernatural invention, protection and assistance in solving problems. Ezra stated boldly that when he fasted and prayed, the Lord answered his prayer petitions (see Ezra 8:21–23).

- Esther the queen fasted for divine protection and supernatural invention against the evil plans of enemy through wicked men and demonic legislation. If we fast for protection, God will deliver us from evil (see Esther 4:16; 5:2).

- Daniel the prophet fasted for 21 days (three whole weeks) for divine breakthrough and for health while seeking the Lord's favor, purpose and vision for his life and God's people (see Daniel 1:5–21; 9:1–27; 10:1–23).

Here are various ways you can fast to experience breakthrough in your life:

- Normal Fast—Abstaining from food but drinking water.

- Absolute Fast—Abstaining from food and water (caution: this fast should not be done for more than three days, and only then if you have clear instruction from God and are in good health).

- Partial Fast—Abstaining from certain kinds of foods
  (no sweets or meats; only soup, fruits and vegetables,
  etc.). Or this could mean fasting from certain meals
  of the day. Daniel did not eat anything desirable or
  any pleasant bread (see Daniel 10:3).
- Smoothie, Liquid or Juice Fast—Fruits and vegetable
  juices only.
- Corporate Fast—Abstaining to pray and intercede.
  Prayer warriors lead believers to fast together for an
  agreed-upon period of time.
- The Jewish Period of Time Fast—Jews would begin
  fasting at 6:00 in the evening and break it the next
  day at 6:00 a.m.

Holy Spirit Fellowship Brings Breakthrough

Communion daily with the Holy Spirit is necessary for believers who say they love Him. The Holy Spirit has been sent
to walk alongside each of us in our Christian journey. He
knows the mind and language of God. It is the Holy Spirit
who equips and empowers us to defeat the works of the
enemy. Mornings with the Holy Spirit will supercharge our
faith and give us the boldness to do all things Christ asks
of us. Jesus was in constant communication with the Lord
in prayer, and He was led constantly by the Spirit of God.
When we commune with the Holy Spirit, God reveals His
secrets to us. "The LORD confides in those who fear him; he
makes his covenant known to them" (Psalm 25:14).

It is as we spend ample time in God's presence that the
secret things of God are revealed to us through the Holy
Spirit. These revealed things break through every invisible

hindrance that is restricting our day (see Deuteronomy 29:29).

The Bible shows that communion was instituted as a way to remember the sacrifice that Christ made when He gave His life for mankind. Communion has been ritualized in most Christian circles, but this was not the intention Christ had in mind when He initiated it. "Do two walk together unless they have agreed to do so?" (Amos 3:3). The Father will meet us halfway when we decide to commune with Him.

I usually set an appointed time to pray with the Father. He always seems to do remarkable things when I meet Him through Holy Spirit engagement (see 1 John 1:3). Here are a few Scripture passages to review concerning communion:

> God is faithful, who has called you into fellowship with his Son, Jesus Christ our Lord.
>
> 1 Corinthians 1:9

> For we were all baptized by one Spirit so as to form one body—whether Jews or Gentiles, slave or free—and we were all given the one Spirit to drink.
>
> 1 Corinthians 12:13

> May the grace of the Lord Jesus Christ, and the love of God, and the fellowship of the Holy Spirit be with you all.
>
> 2 Corinthians 13:14

Praise and Worship Brings Breakthrough

Praise and worship are essential ways to express how we revere and honor God. It is through praise that we can possess the supernatural power to release breakthrough and healing.

David, Paul and Silas saw supernatural release when they activated their praise and worship before the Lord in times of trouble. The breakthrough of Paul and Silas came as a result of their prayers and praise before the Lord while incarcerated. Their worship created an atmosphere of breakthrough for the other prisoners. One person's breakthrough can create an earthquake that others can experience. These times come through praise and worship in God's presence (see Acts 16:25–27).

God used David's music to deliver Saul from tormenting spirits. Praise and worship before the Lord creates a sound of victory and a battle cry in the midst of insurmountable resistance, delay or hindrances. The power of praise and worship can confuse the enemy who is set up against you. Jehoshaphat gathered a group of anointed singers, and through their praise, they became a weapon of confusion and sudden defeat against the enemy.

> After consulting the people, Jehoshaphat appointed men to sing to the LORD and to praise him for the splendor of his holiness as they went out at the head of the army, saying: "Give thanks to the LORD, for his love endures forever." As they began to sing and praise, the LORD set ambushes against the men of Ammon and Moab and Mount Seir who were invading Judah, and they were defeated.
>
> 2 Chronicles 20:21–22

Once all of these tools are applied to your spiritual walk, you are more than able to overcome any setbacks. I have come to realize that past victories or small wins should not be overlooked. Being grateful and celebrating what God has already done for you will better position you to receive present and future victories and spiritual breakthroughs in Christ.

Praise Defined

The word *praise* means "to boast, to rave (about), to commend, to speak well of, to laud or confess."[2] It means to be grateful or thankful for the Lord's blessings and to publish the Gospel of the good news of God to others.[3]

Here are some examples in the Word of God:

- We are to praise the Lord for what He has done for us (see Psalm 6; Psalm 7; 9:1–2; 18:2–3; 28:2).
- We are to praise the Lord for His goodness, grace and mercy (see Psalm 79:13).
- We are to offer up the sacrifice of praise to the Lord with thanksgiving with the fruit of our lips, and we are to present ourselves as a living sacrifice (see Hebrews 13:15; Romans 12:1).
- We are to use our faith in God, which naturally leads us to offer up praises (see 1 Peter 1:7).
- We are to praise during trouble. While incarcerated at midnight, Paul and Silas began to sing praises to God. They prayed and witnessed to other prisoners under the most restricted and isolated circumstances (see Acts 16:25).

Worship Defined

Worship is expressed by prostrating oneself, bowing down, lying facedown before God while paying homage and respect. In other words, worship is the highest form of adoration, service, honor and respect that believers can display toward the Lord. Worship is different from someone praising God. It is a direct conversation between you and God. It involves intimacy and submission to the Lord. It is all about your heart posture and attitude.

Here are some examples in the Word of God:

- We do not worship with man's ways or methods, but we worship God from the heart (see Isaiah 29:13).
- True worship of the Lord places Him first in a believer's life. Jesus restates this when He quotes the greatest commandment from the Old Testament (see Matthew 22:35–40; Luke 17:15–16; 7:36–38).
- Believers are to worship the Father in spirit and in truth (see John 4:23–24).
- We are warned not to worship creation versus the Creator God (see Romans 1:25).

In the life of the believer, worship should be viewed with great importance. Satan knew this, which is why he made it his final temptation attempt to Jesus in the wilderness (see Matthew 4:8–10). What or whom you worship is what or whom you will follow, serve and honor. Worship is not just an emotional experience. It goes beyond words and feelings. It is a core value and foundation for all who are called to be true servants of the Lord. Intimacy is connected to worship because it defines our relationship and alignment with God. There is nothing on this earth or in our lives that is more important than our relationship with God. "Who will separate us from the love of Christ? Will tribulation, or trouble, or persecution, or famine, or nakedness, or danger, or sword?" (Romans 8:35 NASB). His love toward us cannot be removed by anything in this world.

6

Contending with God for Your Breakthrough in Specific Areas

The One who breaks open the way will go up before them; they will break through the gate and go out. Their King will pass through before them, the LORD at their head.

Micah 2:13

There are things in life that we are required to fight for or defend. I have come to realize that our breakthrough will often begin after a season of testing. The Lord will allow His people to be tested right before their breakthrough begins. On the other hand, the enemy will come along to tempt us when we are on the verge of one of our greatest breakthrough seasons. These temptations are the trying of our faith in Christ.

Jesus understood every weakness of ours, because He was tempted in every way on earth (see Hebrews 4:15). He was also tested by the Father, who led Him to the wilderness to be tempted for forty days and nights by a subtle and cunning enemy (see Matthew 4:1–11). We must discern spiritually whom and what we are contending against. The word *contend* means "to strive or vie in contest or rivalry or against difficulties."[1]

Breaking the Cycles

As believers, we find ourselves in various types of battles with the enemy. Biblical examples include striving against opposition as in a battle (see Deuteronomy 2:9), with horses (see Jeremiah 12:5), orally (see Nehemiah 13:11) or spiritually (see Isaiah 57:16). Coping with our flesh, mind, will and emotions will not change the circumstances. But contending with the Lord by His Spirit's power and Word will help us win this invisible struggle between good and evil. This struggle is not accomplished by human strength or power, but by the Spirit of the Lord (see Zechariah 4:6). God will help us break the irregular, illicit and illegal repeated cycles that are stopping our advancement!

These unpredictable challenges might have you questioning yourself. You might ask how you got in this situation in the first place, or you may be fighting in a war of which you are unaware. There is an invisible force of evil sent to block you at every turn to keep you from moving into your destiny and purpose. In addition, there could be word curses sent as fiery darts to keep you bound to your past and to keep you from your future. In the spiritual realm, curses are like darts that are looking for a place to land. As long as you stay away from sin, without the Lord's permission, no one can curse you (see Numbers 22:12, 38; 23:8, 20, 23).

You are a curse breaker by the power of God in you. When you experience any unexpected resistance, attacks or unusual obstacles, your breakthrough is near. You are getting closer to experiencing the fullness and bliss of blessings that are on the other side of the resistance.

This fight that you are engaged in is all about your spiritual breakthrough in Christ to fulfill your prophetic destiny. The enemy is putting up a fight with you, because you are called to discern, disarm, disengage and dismantle him by defeating his evil employment. God will do great exploits to topple the kingdom of darkness with the power of the Holy Spirit (see Daniel 11:32). The strategy of the evil one—the devil—presents itself only when God's people are on the brink of a major breakthrough. I call this turning point a *defining moment*.

This defining moment could be a major opportunity, dream, move, promotion, blessing, vision, increase, favor, etc. You have been praying, fasting, anticipating and waiting for this moment to come. Suddenly, you can sense that something is resisting you in a specific area. Seeing the unexpected starting to happen is an indication that the devil is working overtime to frustrate you, your season and your blessings. He knows that if he can throw off your focus and cause you to disengage emotionally, he has the advantage. His plan is to throw you into a downward spiral of emotions so that you will then make unwise decisions. He wants you to become distracted, embarrassed, ashamed, ridiculed, angry or frustrated.

He is attacking your mind, which is where spiritual warfare begins. The invisible battlefront is the stronghold of our mind (see 2 Corinthians 10:4). We are to guard our thoughts and allow creativity to flow. We need the wisdom of God in this spiritual battle to contend for our breakthrough. We need to understand the rules of spiritual engagement so that we are able to discern what is working against us. The enemy is a war strategist; however, he only comes at us with the same regiment of attacks.

Winning the Invisible Battle

The devil is out to kill, steal and destroy the eternal purposes and will of God for your life (see John 10:10). You must protect and value your spiritual gifts and your mind by any means necessary. One of the enemy's cunning war tactics is to cause God's people to walk in pride. He knows that the Lord will resist the proud and give grace to those who humble themselves (see James 4:6). There is nothing as awful as the Lord resisting you receiving your breakthrough. Always check your heart to make sure that pride does not take root. I am not saying this to alarm you, but I must share biblical truth to inform you that this spiritual battle is real.

The devil does not play by the rules, but we must through God's Word. The life of a believer is a life called to war and to arms in God's Kingdom. Our breakthrough comes when we pray through. We can breach the enemy's line every time when we understand the spiritual art of war. I will not go fully into details regarding the rules of engagement in discerning, disarming and defeating the works of the enemy, but if you are interested, you can read my book *Unseen Warfare*. For now, I want to show you how to contend with God in this battle for victory in specific areas of your life.

For though we live in the flesh, we do not wage war according to the flesh. The weapons of our warfare are not the weapons of the world. Instead, they have divine power to demolish strongholds. We tear down arguments and every presumption set up against the knowledge of God; and we take captive every thought to make it obedient to Christ.

2 Corinthians 10:3–5 BSB

The weapons believers fight with are not worldly weapons—they are spiritual ones. They have divine supernatural power to demolish strongholds. In addition, they have the power to help us break through any invisible barrier set up by the enemy. It is the strategy of the enemy to cause God's people to walk in the flesh and not in the spirit (see Galatians 5:16). If believers yield to the works of the flesh, they hinder their own spiritual progress.

Supernaturally Armed

Do not become the enemy's puppet that is controlled and seduced by the lust of the eyes, the lust of the flesh and the pride of life (see 1 John 2:16). You must become fully prepared to fight back with the authority and power of God against any onslaught of temptation, deception or false accusation. "Finally, be strong in the Lord and in his mighty power. Put on the full armor of God, so that you can take your stand against the devil's schemes" (Ephesians 6:10–11).

The apostle Paul encourages believers to be strong in their faith and to be confident in the power of the Lord's might. To contend in this spiritual battle against evil, we are to be fully clad with God's armor. We are charged to put on the whole armor—not just some of it. Paul says that if we put on His armor when evil presents itself, we are able to stand our ground (see Ephesians 6:13).

Girding ourselves with the armor of God will give us the advantage and the posture to stand in the face of adversity when it comes. It is better to be prepared than to be unprepared or unaware. Believers can contend with the invisible adversary when they are spiritually equipped and suited with the six pieces of God's armor found in Ephesians 6:13–18:

1. Belt of truth
2. Breastplate of righteousness
3. Shoes of peace
4. Shield of faith
5. Helmet of salvation
6. Sword of the Spirit

Having these six pieces of the armor of God will assist every believer in winning the invisible battle that rages in the unseen realm. The armor that we possess is not an armor that is created by man or by a natural military force. It is God's armor, and we can use it to stand against the evil one. The devil is after six things:

1. Stopping the truth of God's Word from operating in a believer's life (see 1 John 4:6).
2. Keeping the righteousness of God from functioning in a believer's life (see Psalm 33:18–22; Romans 5:16–17).
3. Blocking the peace of God from being present in a believer's life (see Isaiah 26:3; John 14:27; Philippians 4:7).
4. Hindering faith to possess Kingdom belief systems that operate in a believer's life—joy, peace

and righteousness in the Holy Spirit (see Romans 14:17).

5. Stopping the salvation of God or deliverance from the kingdom of darkness into the Kingdom of Light from being active in a believer's life (see Colossians 1:13).

6. Keeping the Word of God from anchoring a believer's life (*logos*—written; *rhema*—spoken word) (see Matthew 4:4; Luke 4:4, 8, 12).

The spiritual warfare in which believers engage to receive breakthrough includes the six areas mentioned above. If you, for example, received a prophetic word that God has called you to fulfill something great in your generation, the enemy will come to challenge the truth that it was spoken prophetically over you. He will challenge whether or not it was a genuine prophetic word. In addition, he will attempt to cause you to walk in doubt, unbelief and uncertainty as to what the Father declared.

The ploy of the devil is to seduce believers with a more lucrative and appealing offer than suffering with Christ (see 1 Corinthians 15:3; John 15:18–20; 1 Peter 4:17–19; Matthew 5:11–12; Romans 8:17). When we find ourselves in a cycle of constant attack, or we say to ourselves that we are always experiencing trouble, I believe that we must look beyond the natural landscape. We should look beneath the surface and discern that there is an invisible nemesis who opposes everything that we are called to do.

Power to Restrict and Revoke

God is trying to get our attention to keep us from sinking in defeat because of the barrage of attacks unleashed against us. "Be sober, be vigilant; because your adversary the devil, as a roaring lion, walketh about, seeking whom he may devour" (1 Peter 5:8 KJV). The Word of God goes on to say that we are to be alert and sober minded in prayer (see 1 Peter 1:13; 4:7). The Bible is clear that God's people do not perish because of sickness, disease, poverty, demonic spirits or division. God's people perish due to lack of knowledge (see Hosea 4:6). Believers do not realize how much Holy Spirit power they possess. The Lord stated that His people perish because of ignorance and the lack of knowledge to be able to educate themselves with the truth. If a person does not know their enemy and his plan of attack against them, they will lose the battle every time.

We are made alive with Christ through our decision to align and agree with the truth of God. Believers of Christ can contend for their breakthrough in specific areas by restricting and revoking the plans of the enemy in those areas. We have to restrict the restrictor and revoke him of his limited power. "I have given you authority to trample on snakes and scorpions and to overcome all the power of the enemy; nothing will harm you" (Luke 10:19). The Father has given His people authority over all the powers of the enemy. Not some, but all.

We have revoking and restricting power by God through the Holy Spirit, and we have it through Jesus, who is the Strong Man. He is able to bind Satan and plunder his goods, which are the souls of men. The enemy is after our soul, and he wants to hold us hostage to the old sin nature (see John 17:15; Luke 4:18; Ephesians 4:8). Satan is very strong, and he watches and guards his possessions jealously. Jesus, however, is stronger. He can arrest him, take his spoils and deliver us from his grip. When the Father sent Jesus to earth to save humanity, it was a rescue mission (see John 3:16; 12:31; Luke 11:21–22). Contending against the plan of the enemy should not be our primary focus, because Jesus already defeated him on the cross (see Colossians 2:15).

You are not exempt or the exception to the rules of engagement released against you by the enemy. To *revoke* the enemy is "to put an end to the validity or operation of a decree, decision, or promise."[2] And to *restrict* him is "to put a limit on or keep under control."[3] God has put all things in subjection under Jesus' feet, and He made Him head over the Church and all things.

We are the Body of Christ. As a part of that Body, with Jesus as the Head, we are able to put demonic resistance under our feet. Jesus is far above all principalities, powers, might and dominion. He is above every name that is named, not only in this world, but also in that world that is to come (see Ephesians 1:20–22). Followers of Christ can contend for breakthrough with God as King and Lord of the breakthrough. All authority in heaven and on earth has been given to Jesus. As His subjects, ambassadors, co-heirs and followers, we have been given delegated authority in the earth and over the works of God's hands (see Psalm 8:6; Matthew 28:18; 2 Corinthians 5:20; Philippians 2:9).

Whether your breakthrough is spiritual, physical, mental, emotional, financial or economic, the way to contend with the Lord for spiritual breakthrough and victory is to:

- Resist the devil and he will flee (see James 4:7).
- Be strong in the Lord and in the power of His might (see Ephesians 6:10).
- Be sober minded, alert, and vigilant (see 1 Peter 5:8).

- Be obedient to God's Word by hearing His voice (see Deuteronomy 5:33; 1 Kings 19:12; Acts 5:29).
- Be fully suited with God's armor (see Ephesians 6).
- Fast and pray (see Joel 2:12; Mark 9:29).
- Watch and pray (see Matthew 26:41).
- Know and study the Word of God (see 2 Timothy 2:15).
- Be submitted to spiritual authority and accountable to other believers (see Hebrews 13:7; Romans 13:1; Acts 20:28).
- Pray without ceasing and pray in the Holy Spirit (speaking in other tongues) (see 1 Thessalonians 5:17; Ephesians 6:18; Jude 1:20; Romans 8:26–27).
- Participate in prophetic warfare (see 1 Timothy 1:18).
- Walk in the spirit of truth (see John 14:15–26; Galatians 5:16–25).
- Walk in the fruit of the Holy Spirit (see Galatians 5:22–24).
- Praise and worship (see 2 Chronicles 20:22).
- Walk in faith and not fear (see 2 Corinthians 5:7; Isaiah 41:10).
- Become a giver, a sower and one who tithes (see Genesis 14:19–20, 26:12; Luke 6:38; Acts 20:35).

Healing Power of Breakthrough Faith

As we partner with the Holy Spirit in holy communion, we are able to outwit and outmatch the enemy. Without God's help, this wrestling match would cause believers to tap out and wave the white flag of surrender; however, God will supernaturally equip His people to win the fight. We are not called to bind or rebuke the enemy, but to resist him and watch him flee (see James 4:7). Only Jesus can issue and enforce an arrest warrant on the strongman—the devil—for harassing and tormenting those who are called to inherit the Kingdom of God. We revoke and restrict the enemy by exercising our spiritual rights and authority and by knowing the power we possess in the Holy Spirit.

The enemy will attempt to attack believers with a plague of attacks that will be emotional, physical or psychological. In the physical realm, the plagues can be sickness, disease or terminal illnesses. Since our physical bodies are the temple of the Holy Spirit (see 1 Corinthians 6:19), we host the healing power of God. The same Spirit who raised Christ from the dead is hosted by believers (see Romans 8:11).

I am reminded of the woman who had an issue of blood for twelve years. She came to Jesus in faith to receive healing power. She thought to herself that if she could just touch the hem of His garment, she would be made whole. She aligned her faith and her heart to the healing power of Jesus, and she received her healing by making a prophetic decree. "For she said within herself, If I may but touch his garment, I shall be whole" (Matthew 9:21 KJV). In faith she acted upon what she declared for herself. She touched the hem of Jesus' garment, and virtue came out of Him and flowed into her. Her hemorrhaging of blood stopped (see Luke 8:43–48).

Then there is the story of the crippled man who received healing breakthrough after waiting for 38 years (see John 5). Jesus spoke a word of faith, telling him to take up his bed and walk. Faith already existed in both the crippled man at the Pool of Bethesda and the woman with the issue of blood. They both, however, needed to walk in their faith to receive what they had been anticipating. The enemy wants to ensnare and entice you with things that are contrary to God's will and Word. He wants you to take the bait and fall prey to his threats.

> And the Lord's servant must not be quarrelsome but must be kind to everyone, able to teach, not resentful. Opponents must be gently instructed, in the hope that God will grant them repentance leading them to a knowledge of the truth, and that they will come to their senses and escape from the trap of the devil, who has taken them captive to do his will.
>
> 2 Timothy 2:24–26

Truth Is a Deliverer

The Lord's servants must discern the enemy's war plans, which are to have God's people do his bidding. The enemy's will is the opposite of the Lord's. Deliverance and healing are needed in specific areas in order for believers to encounter daily breakthrough, freedom and victory. The Bible says that deliverance is the children's bread (see Matthew 15:26).

Breakthrough and deliverance are a part of our spiritual inheritance. The enemy attacks our minds with deception, hoping that we will abandon the journey God wants to take us on. If the enemy can keep us bound and focus all our attention on past hurts, disappointments, failures, sin, sickness, disease, guilt, shame, unforgiveness, bad relationships, mistakes and mishaps, then we will never encounter deliverance. Our faith in God will help us contend with the Lord for our breakthrough.

> Count it all joy, my brothers, when you meet trials of various kinds, for you know that the testing of your faith produces

steadfastness. And let steadfastness have its full effect, that
you may be perfect and complete, lacking in nothing.

James 1:2–4 ESV

Freedom involves activating the Word of God in our lives
so that we can rescue and deliver others. Deliverance is more
than driving out evil spirits that are invading people's lives.
Deliverance is being rescued from the deceptive measures of
the enemy. Our understanding of the truth in God's Word
and the decisions that we make based on that understanding
will set us free. Jesus said, "And you will know the truth, and
the truth will set you free" (John 8:32 NLT). Sin becomes the
master of those who succumb to it. The power of deliverance
and freedom is in the spirit of truth and the revelation that
you are free in Christ.

7

Planning for Breakthrough Every Day

The plans of the diligent lead surely to abundance, but everyone who is hasty comes only to poverty.

Proverbs 21:5 ESV

Every day, breakthrough and miracles should be our aim and our expectation. We can lean into God's heart and hear His plans for our future. "'For I know the plans I have for you,' declares the LORD, 'plans to prosper you and not to harm you, plans to give you hope and a future'" (Jeremiah 29:11). The Lord knows exactly what He has created you to do in the earth, and you have a part to play in the Lord's plan to permeate the message of the Kingdom from our communities to the far corners of the earth (see Matthew 24:14).

The world says that we should follow our heart, but the Father wills the pursuit of holiness in a believer's life. We are to follow after God's heart and align our heart to His. Faithfulness and holiness are important pieces of the Lord's plan for our lives as His children. These pieces reflect who we are becoming in Christ Jesus. Knowing and acknowledging God's plans will allow Him to direct and order our steps toward breakthrough success, victory and transformation in every area. Perseverance and breakthrough are two key components in a believer's spiritual walk. "You need to persevere so that when you have done the will of God, you will receive what he has promised" (Hebrews 10:36).

God's Plan for Breakthrough

Waiting and cooperating with God's timing with a plan in mind will move your breakthrough toward you, or it will navigate you toward it. The Lord wants His people to be deliberate in their faith even in the midst of setbacks, trials and daily tribulation. I believe we can plan and command to see breakthrough in our lives when we are steadfast and consistent and when we endure and persevere. "The characteristic of a man who is not swerved from his deliberate purpose and his loyalty to faith and piety by even the greatest trials and sufferings."[1] Those who will seek and hear God's voice daily by being led of His Spirit are children of breakthrough (see Romans 8:14).

King David's prayer to the Lord was, "Teach me your way, LORD, that I may rely on your faithfulness; give me an undivided heart, that I may fear your name" (Psalm 86:11). God's love language is found in His Word; therefore, knowing His will and planning our day in expectation of the unexpected is living by faith and not by sight (see 2 Corinthians 5:7; Proverbs 3:5–6). "This is the confidence we have in approaching

God: that if we ask anything according to his will, he hears us. And if we know that he hears us—whatever we ask—we know that we have what we asked of him" (1 John 5:14–15).

When you trust God's plan for your life, you can plan for breakthrough, healing, miracles, favor, deliverance, wholeness, freedom, restoration and financial provision to fulfill your calling. The Father will remove any timidity, fear, doubt and uncertainty that comes to you when you pursue His will. The Lord will clear your path so that you can gain momentum as you trust and acknowledge Him in all your ways (see Proverbs 3:5–6).

Regardless of any intense opposition we might experience, God's plans will prevail. The Lord says, "Surely, as I have planned, so it will be, and as I have purposed, so it will happen" (Isaiah 14:24). There are those God already had in mind who will become conformed to the image of His Son through their walk with Him.

> And we know that God works all things together for the good of those who love Him, who are called according to His purpose. For those God foreknew, He also predestined to be conformed to the image of His Son, so that He would be the firstborn among many brothers. And those He predestined, He also called; those He called, He also justified; those He justified, He also glorified.
>
> Romans 8:28–30 BSB

Ultimately, the Father's will for you will outweigh any daily struggle, mishap, unexpected obstacle or resistance that you encounter. The Lord's eternal purpose for you is that you prosper and have hope and a future. His plan for you is not one of calamity, uncertainty, destruction or hopelessness.

His is a plan of welfare, hope, joy, peace and breakthrough in every area of your life. You can schedule your day in God's presence.

You can write out your prophetic decrees, daily confessions, Scripture verses and action plans to do His will. The Lord does not want you to schedule around Him. He wants you to put Him in your schedule. You do not know what tomorrow will bring, but that should not keep you from planning your day with a vision to seek the Kingdom (see Psalm 27:1; James 4:13–14; Matthew 6:33–34).

Do you have a vision and a plan for your life? Do you know what is the will of the Lord concerning you? He knows your beginning and ending. Who is better suited to lead you into what lies ahead? In the Old Testament, the Lord instructed His prophets to write everything He spoke as His intent or will. They heard God's prophetic decrees and recorded them all on tablets or scrolls. Their ears were spiritually aligned to His voice, and they prophesied what they heard (see Ezekiel 37:7; 2 Peter 1:21).

Plan Your Plans

The words they heard, wrote and spoke were aligned and in agreement with God's words that echoed from His throne room. God, for instance, put His Word in Jeremiah's and Isaiah's mouths (see Isaiah 51:6; Jeremiah 1:9). And Romans tells us, "For everything that was written in the past was written to teach us, so that through the endurance taught in the Scriptures and the encouragement they provide we might have hope" (Romans 15:4). Even John wrote down what he saw and what he heard as the Lord revealed it to him (see Revelation 1:19).

They were able to write and record what the Lord's plan was. You, too, can plan your day by hearing His voice directing you. "Whether you turn to the right or to the left, your ears will hear a voice behind you, saying, 'This is the way; walk in it'" (Isaiah 30:21).

I believe that journaling is a powerful tool to use to plan your days. Journaling is a written record of your feelings, thoughts and intentions. There are no specific rules on how to do it, although most journaling is a daily exercise. It is a great method to track everyday life. Whether we call it note taking, journaling or writing in a diary or a planner, they are all great options. We will see amazing benefits when we follow through and write down what we are hearing and seeing.

Mary would treasure moments and events surrounding Jesus' birth, and she pondered them in her heart (see Luke 2:19). The psalmist declares, "Great are the works of the LORD; they are pondered by all who delight in them" (Psalm 111:2). The prophet Habakkuk said:

> Then the LORD answered me: "Write down this vision and clearly inscribe it on tablets, so that a herald may run with it. For the vision awaits an appointed time; it testifies of the end and does not lie. Though it lingers, wait for it, since it will surely come and will not delay."
>
> Habakkuk 2:2–3 BSB

This is clearly planning and writing out your life's objectives, goals, agendas and vision. Planning for breakthrough spiritually and naturally can only be accomplished when we align our will to God's will. Planning should be our practice, discipline and exercise. Doing so will allow us to monitor our spiritual progression. In addition, we are able to navigate and discern what options are best when things do not go as we have planned. Our vision must be legible and clear enough for ourselves and others to read it and fulfill it. There is an appointed time for fulfillment, but we must be patient. It will not delay. The enemy, however, also has a plan concerning you. It is to kill, steal and destroy (see John 10:10).

We can live a purpose-driven life. Believers have the ability and the power to command their morning. Command our morning? What does that mean? To command your morning is not suggesting that you are giving God orders. It means that we should take full responsibility over our day under His direction and supervision. Have you found yourself hitting the ground running, but come quickly to the realization that something is amiss?

I believe that we are called to plan our day and antici-pate God's goodness as we seek Him in prayer. What do you want your day to look like? Do you know what you are destined by God to do, and are you walking fully in it? Are you waiting on a prayer to be answered? Are you waking up purposeless and unaware of what the Lord has created you to do? Whatever the reason or excuse that you might have, you are still called to plan and command your breakthrough each and every day.

Planning is a biblical principle. The Word of God shares that an individual who plans well will be able to foresee dangers and avoid them (see Proverbs 22:3). The foolish, however, will rush ahead unprepared and do whatever is convenient at the time. Those who plan and fulfill those plans possess wisdom. Those who do not plan walk aimlessly and blindly, and they end up paying the penalty for their lack of planning. No one builds a home without a blueprint, and we cannot have a sure foundation and solid financial structure without a plan.

Plan and Command Your Day

Are you planning and commanding your morning or day with the Word of God and the prophetic spoken word? Are you aligning your plans with God's plan in His Word?

What does it mean to command your morning? Is this even biblical to do? I love what the Bible says about commanding the morning: "Have you commanded the morning since your days began, and caused the dawn to know its place, that it might take hold of the skirts of the earth, and the wicked be shaken out of it?" (Job 38:12–13 ESV). God is challenging Job as it pertains to His mighty power and our ability to decree in His authority.

God has given you delegated power and authority to order your day to align itself to His will. You have the commanding power by the Holy Spirit to organize your day to bring you what you have been seeking. You can plan your healing breakthrough, miracle breakthrough, deliverance breakthrough, financial breakthrough, spiritual breakthrough and more! There is no limit to what you can do by aligning your words and decrees to God's will and purpose.

You can walk His words out daily without fear, intimidation or doubt. Jesus planned daily to walk in the purpose that He was sent to the earth to accomplish. The will of the Father became Jesus' daily nourishment, meat or food. "Jesus saith unto them, My meat is to do the will of him that sent me, and to finish his work" (John 4:34 KJV). Furthermore, Jesus reveals the perfect alignment: "For I have come down from heaven, not to do My own will, but to do the will of Him who sent Me" (John 6:38 BSB).

God establishes our plans when we are faithful to Him. "Commit to the LORD whatever you do, and he will establish your plans" (Proverbs 16:3). Mornings, evenings and nights with the Holy Spirit are imperative in our spiritual walk and development. Breakthroughs should become commonplace in the life of the believer. One of the things that I have found in my Christian walk is that when I am not consistent in my devotional time and prayer life, my day is off and is misaligned. Consistency is key when it comes to communicating with the Lord. It is in the secret place of prayer that we are given details concerning how to handle toxic relationships and spiritual hindrances.

Believers should write and speak out daily decrees, breakthrough confessions and Scripture verses. Planning and commanding your day with specific and targeted prayers, decrees and Scripture passages is a simple, yet very powerful spiritual technique that will allow you to activate greater authority over your day. It will help you to be able to pinpoint any demonic or unseen interference, inception and interruption.

Planning assists with starting your day off right and setting the tone. It activates and establishes God's Word in your life. Commanding your morning is not about praying specific prayers, but it is about actually applying the Word of God by speaking and prophesying over your day. This includes daily confessions, declarations, decrees or affirmations.

People are to use Bible verses to order their morning, afternoon, evening or night—whatever time they choose. The Hebrew word for command is *tsâvâh*, which means "to lay charge (upon), give charge (to), command, order," and it is used 494 times in the Old Testament.[2] This word implies an authoritative order or directive.

How to Align Your Day

Believers can command (give authoritative, biblical and spiritual orders) their morning and lives. Planning and commanding your morning may be a new concept to you, but it is biblical and so powerful. Jesus said that we can do greater things than what He did (see John 14:12).

In the book of Job, the Lord assigned His lovingkindness to show up in the daytime by His command (see Job 38:12). He ordered the morning to set in motion His lovingkindness. Job, in fact, could command his morning. Believers today can do so as well. If believers desire to have the light of God's Kingdom shine upon their ways, they should first be in right standing with the Lord (see Psalm 119:105).

They can then command their day by making a decree, and it will be established (see Job 22:28). What they decree should be in line with the will and truth of God's Word for their lives. Believers have the spiritual authority to choose how they will use their words every single day. Our tongues possess the power to release life into our day when we plan and command our morning (see Proverbs 18:21).

Below is a simple example of powerful decree, declaration, prayer point and Scripture confession that you can speak over yourself to command your day for supernatural breakthrough:

- Proverbs 3:4—You have God and man's favor.
- Isaiah 52:12—The Lord goes before you and becomes your rear guard.

- Psalm 68:19—You are loaded daily with His benefits.
- James 2:23—You are God's friend.

Today, I decree that I have favor with God and man. Father, I am Your friend because of my faithful relationship with You by faith. You go before me and are my rear guard. I am loaded daily with Your benefits. In Jesus' name, Amen! (And it is so!)

I have found that using this practice has an impact on the spiritual victories that I experience. Here are a few tools you will need to plan and command your day:

- A Bible that has room in the margins for notes or other forms of creative expression.
- A notebook/journal to write down notes for decrees, confessions and verses to command your day. It will be useful to keep a running record of all the Scripture verses you find to plan and command your day.
- A Bible app to establish a Scripture-based foundation and to search for specific subject matter to formulate your daily decrees. It will be helpful to search for specific types of verses to command your morning.

The decrees, confessions, prayer points and verses that you use to command your day should be very specific and organized. You can use Post-it tabs within your notebook or journal to keep everything organized. Being organized makes it easier to find Scripture passages, and because of this, I suggest using index cards or Post-it Notes to write out your morning prophetic decrees, declarations, confessions or Scripture verses.

Normally, I use my cell phone notes to write all my personal daily breakthrough decrees that I have created when planning and commanding my day. This way I can take them with me everywhere I go. Also, place your morning commands where you can see them so that you can remind yourself to speak them. Make commanding your morning a routine and daily discipline.

- Be consistent: Make it a habit to write out and speak your daily verses.
- Starting point: Use two or three of your favorite verses and build your decrees from there.
- Incorporate: Add everything concerning you and those you love in your morning decrees.

Part two of the book will assist you as you create or formulate your own personal prayer points, decrees, Scripture passages and daily confessions.

PART
TWO

40 Breakthrough Decrees and Scripture Verses

FRIENDSHIPS

Peer-Level Companionships

Perfume and incense bring joy to the heart, and the pleasantness of a friend springs from their heartfelt advice.

Proverbs 27:9

Today, I decree . . .

- The Lord is surrounding me with divine, peer-level relationships and companions who are honest, genuine, trustworthy, godly, mutually beneficial and long-lasting.
- My friendships are God-given and are with people who will stick closer than a sibling.
- My peer-level relationships will be with those who love God and who pray for and with each other when we are going through difficulties.
- My comrades will not be tainted, perverted or influenced by ungodly voices of wickedness.
- My confidants will be sweet like oil and will be filled with godly wisdom and advice.

Proverbs 18:24; Job 42:10

Greater Love Friendships

Greater love has no one than this, that someone lay down his life for his friends.

John 15:13 ESV

Today, I decree . . .

- I have faithful, mutual friendships with people who will bring a necessary correction or rebuke when needed.
- God is establishing and aligning me with healthy and prosperous friendships with the opposite sex.
- My companions and peers are ethical, moral and spiritual.
- The Father is placing iron-sharpening friendships in my life that will keep me spiritually accountable.
- My comrades will love me unconditionally and will build me up in my faith.

Proverbs 17:17; 27:5–6; 1 Thessalonians 5:11;
Romans 1:12

Love-Covering Courtships

Whoever covers an offense seeks love, but he who repeats a matter separates close friends.

Proverbs 17:9 ESV

Today, I decree . . .

- Every relationship that is hindering or evil will be exposed and will be removed immediately out of my life.
- My heart will be joined together with right relationships that God brings, and I will not be unequally yoked with the wrong ones.
- As an unmarried believer, I will walk in the Spirit and not fulfill any lustful desires or appetites of the flesh while dating.
- My courtship will always represent the image and love of God in word and deed.
- Every toxic relationship, illegal soul tie or fleshly entanglement that has been established is broken and severed.

1 Corinthians 5:11; 2 Corinthians 6:14–15; Galatians 5:16

Wise, Mentoring Relationships

A wise man will hear, and will increase learning; and a man of understanding shall attain unto wise counsels.

Proverbs 1:5 KJV

Today, I decree . . .

- God is ordering my steps to walk with the wise so that I will daily become wiser in my spiritual development and journey.
- I will increase in learning and give ear to the wisdom of God so that I may gain understanding of my purpose on the earth.
- Godly mentors will assist me in my specific calling, and they will train me for spiritual breakthrough in every area.
- The Holy Spirit as the Comforter, Helper, Consultant and Advocate will teach, lead, guide and equip me in what I have been called to do.
- I will submit continually to godly alignments and leadership that will keep me protected and humble.

Proverbs 1:5; 13:20; John 14:26

MARRIAGE

A Unified Marriage

The husband should give to his wife her conjugal rights, and likewise the wife to her husband.

1 Corinthians 7:3 ESV

Today, I decree . . .

- What God has ordained and put together, I will protect from division, hate and jealousy.
- Mutual love, respect and honor will be at the center of this godly union, and we will become inseparable.
- Two is better than one, and we will reap the benefit of our labor.
- No sexual immorality, adultery, spirit of dishonor, disunity, lustful temptation or perversion will enter into this marriage, and any seducing notion is eradicated.
- This marriage is monogamous and divorce-free. It is full of transparency, wholeness and truth.

1 Corinthians 7:2; Ecclesiastes 4:9–12; Colossians 3:18–19

Untainted Union

Let the husband render to his wife the affection due her, and likewise also the wife to her husband.

1 Corinthians 7:3 NKJV

Today, I decree . . .

- I will experience divine breakthrough in every area of my marriage, and I will understand the love language of my spouse.
- God is igniting a new passion and honor between my spouse and me, and the bedchambers will stay undefiled and free from contamination, infidelity or adultery.
- Righteous purity, wholeness and oneness of love for each other will be better than wine in this marriage.
- In this marriage, we both will fulfill each other's marital needs, and we will work to save our marriage according to God's Word.
- This marriage is sanctified, holy and righteous in the sight of the Lord, and there will be renewed love.

Hebrews 13:4; Song of Solomon 4:10; 1 Corinthians 7:3

Honorable Spouses

Let each one of you love his wife as himself, and let the wife see that she respects her husband.

Ephesians 5:33 ESV

Today, I decree . . .

- This marriage will be saturated with the favor of God, and we will display mutual respect, honor, love and faithfulness to each other that will bring happiness.
- God is breaking and exposing every unseen plot, ploy or trick of the enemy that would bring about disloyalty, mistrust, dishonor or unfaithfulness.
- Our biblically supported spousal agreement, marital vows and expectations are upheld daily with the highest regard.
- No weapon formed or forged by the enemy against us will prosper in any way, and our prayers will not be hindered.
- This God-given union will be a symbol and a perfect example of Christ's love for His Bride, the Church.

Isaiah 54:17; Ephesians 5:25–27; 1 Peter 3:7

Healed Hearts

So they are no longer two but one flesh. What therefore God has joined together, let not man separate.

Matthew 19:6 ESV

Today, I decree . . .

- Joy, peace, healing and righteousness will be within my house, marriage, family and every work to which I put my hands.
- The joy of the Lord will be our strength in this marriage, and we will begin to experience unusual breakthroughs and victories in the Holy Spirit.
- In this marriage, we experience financial, mental, physical and spiritual breakthroughs.
- The enemy is giving us back double for our trouble, and God is restoring all that was lost.
- There is nothing lacking, missing, stolen, broken, damaged or destroyed in this marriage. God is healing any unresolved wounds and is restoring total health.

Nehemiah 8:10; Jeremiah 30:17; James 4:1

FAMILY

Extended Relatives

But if anyone does not provide for his relatives, and especially for members of his household, he has denied the faith and is worse than an unbeliever.

1 Timothy 5:8 ESV

Today, I decree . . .

- The Father is enlarging my borders and territory while increasing me and my extended family with breakthrough blessings.
- I will provide for those I love and those who are a part of my household that the Lord will see my faith and bless me.
- God is placing divine connections in my sphere of activity. He is giving me people I consider family who will pray for, support and love me.
- I will not walk alone in this season. The Father is aligning me with those who have my best interests at heart and with whom I have all things in common.
- This is a season of total recovery and restoration. Blessings will follow for my household and for everyone who is connected to me.

1 Chronicles 4:10; Acts 2:44

Crown Jewels

Behold, children are a heritage from the LORD, the fruit of the womb a reward.

Psalm 127:3 ESV

Today, I decree . . .

- I will lay up an inheritance for my children's children, and the wealth of the wicked will be transferred to me.
- Everything is working together for me and my children's good, because I am called according to God's purpose and I love Him.
- I will be fruitful, increase in number, reproduce, fill the earth and subdue it as God's spiritual representative on earth.
- I will train and raise up the next generation, including my children, in the ways of the Lord so that they will not turn away from the Father when they are old.
- My children will call me blessed of the Lord, and the crowned glory of children is their guardianship.

Isaiah 54:13; Genesis 1:28; Proverbs 22:6

Household of Faith

Remember your leaders, those who spoke to you the word of God. Consider the outcome of their way of life, and imitate their faith.

Hebrews 13:7 ESV

Today, I decree . . .

- My church family and community is vibrant, powerful and anointed by God with the glory that brings breakthrough, healing, wholeness, deliverance, restoration and the supernatural.
- As I am planted in the household of faith and am submitted to other faithful believers, I will flourish, prosper and receive what the Father has destined for me.
- The Father is giving me pastors and leaders who are after His heart who will skillfully lead, guide and feed me as God has instructed them.
- Supernatural breakthrough, favor and unity will be resident in the house of God, and dissension, division, competition, quarreling, hate and disunity will be exposed and removed.
- Today I have clear vision and prophetic guidance by the Holy Spirit for my life.

Jeremiah 3:15; Proverbs 11:14; Psalm 78:72

WORK, BUSINESS, CAREER

Greatest Employee

It shall not be so among you. But whoever would be great among you must be your servant.

Matthew 20:26 ESV

Today, I decree . . .

- I will respect my employers as the Bible instructs, and I will find favor in the sight of the Lord.
- The wisdom of God will direct my words and deeds while dealing with a harsh manager, supervisor or employer.
- My workplace atmosphere will be free from gossip, slander, deceit, evil practices and plots against me.
- My words spoken daily at work will be laced with a gentle answer that will deflect anger from those over me.
- I will walk in the spirit of honor, submission and humility, and the Lord will promote me in due season.

Proverbs 15:1; Hebrews 13:17; 1 Peter 2:18–20

Marketplace Entrepreneurs

Whatever you do, work heartily, as for the Lord and not for men.

Colossians 3:23 ESV

Today, I decree . . .

- My financial and spiritual gifts will make room for me and bring me into the presence of great men who will provide necessary resources, investments, favor, opportunities and financial breakthroughs as the Lord directs.
- I will write the vision and make it clear so that others will read it and run with it to fulfill my God-given dream.
- My influence is increasing, and the Lord is providing wisdom that will protect my assets, investments, marketplace relationships and partnerships.
- As I commit my business plans, goals, objectives, vision and concepts to the Lord, He will establish them.
- As I put my hands to the plow, I am supernaturally strengthened by God and fit to experience divine harvest and financial longevity in every area.

Habakkuk 2:2–4; Psalm 37:5; Luke 9:62

Employees' Favor

For we are co-workers in God's service; you are God's field, God's building.

1 Corinthians 3:9

Today, I decree . . .

- I will lead by example among my co-workers in the workplace as I display the love of Christ.
- I can do all things through Christ, who strengthens me when I am weak and unable to cope with day-to-day duties at work.
- Every unseen warfare that comes to frustrate me will be put to an end, and the Lord will fight my battles.
- There is breakthrough favor among my employees, and the Lord is preparing a table in the presence of my enemies.
- I will be steadfast, immovable, always abounding in the work of the Lord, knowing that my labor is not in vain, even at work among my co-workers.

1 Corinthians 15:58; Psalm 23:5; Philippians 4:13

The Father's Business

And if you have not been faithful in that which is another's,
who will give you that which is your own?

Luke 16:12 ESV

Today, I decree . . .

- I will be about my Father's business and will fulfill my spiritual obligation and calling in the earth.
- When I am faithful over a few things, God will make me ruler over many things.
- Financial blessings, provision and favor are all around me and within my borders.
- The Kingdom of God is advancing through me as the Body of Christ, and everything to which I put my hands will prosper as I am obedient to God's Word.
- As I prosper in my business, I will honor the Lord with my substance and sow the firstfruits of my increase so that there are continual blessings, divine protection and an open heaven.

Proverbs 3:9–10; Luke 2:49; Matthew 25:21

SPIRITUAL HEALTH

Forgiving Attitude

Be kind to one another, tenderhearted, forgiving one another, as God in Christ forgave you.

Ephesians 4:32 ESV

Today, I decree . . .

- I will not walk in unforgiveness, bitterness, resentment, guilt, shame or condemnation.
- I will make the decision to let go and forgive any past or present hurt, pain or grudges created by others.
- I will forgive as the Lord forgave me of my offenses and wrongdoings, and I will learn to forgive myself in the process.
- I will not allow the spirit of offense to rob me of what is rightfully mine in God's Word. In obedience, I will continue to release festering issues and burdens to the Lord.
- As I confess my sins daily, knowing that the Lord is just to forgive me, I will extend that same mercy to pardon others. I will ask others to forgive me for the wrongdoings I have committed against them.

James 5:16; Colossians 3:13

Spiritual Hunger

As the deer pants for streams of water, so my soul pants for you, my God. My soul thirsts for God, for the living God.

Psalm 42:1–2

Today, I decree . . .

- I will hunger and thirst after righteousness and will not be moved by any sudden, unseen distraction or hindrance.
- My meat is to do the will of the Father, and as an obedient child of God, I will finish His work.
- Every diabolical plot, scheme, trick or invisible warfare against my prayer life and devotional time in God's presence will be stopped immediately.
- My passion and commitment to the Word of God, prayer, fasting, studying and worship will increase, and every unseen blockage will be exposed.
- As I delight myself in God's presence, the desires of my heart will be met.

Psalm 37:4–5; Matthew 5:6; John 4:34

Holy Spirit Communion

May the grace of the Lord Jesus Christ, and the love of God, and the fellowship of the Holy Spirit be with you all.

2 Corinthians 13:14

Today, I decree . . .

- The Holy Spirit will reveal the mind, will and purpose of God for my life for me to fulfill.
- I am moving in the timing of God and cooperating with the Holy Spirit to experience perpetual breakthrough in every area of my life.
- Every preventing, prohibiting, hindering or blocking stronghold is being cast down, and I have joy, peace and righteousness in the Holy Spirit.
- Brand-new mercies come to me, and the grace and love of the Father is extended to me with daily benefits.
- My spiritual gifts are being sharpened, and the Holy Spirit is bringing the truth of God's Word to me as I seek the Father.

Psalm 68:19; 2 Corinthians 10:5

Revelation of God

The secret things belong to the LORD our God, but the things that are revealed belong to us and to our children forever, that we may do all the words of this law.

Deuteronomy 29:29 ESV

Today, I decree . . .

- I will receive fresh revelation of the Father's heart, and I will align myself with His Word. I will receive my portion.
- I am more than a conqueror through Christ, who loves me, and I will receive daily breakthroughs.
- God is making the impossible possible, because all things are possible with the Father.
- My heart will remain pure before the Lord, and He will continue to reveal Himself to me.
- I will seek the Kingdom of God and the Father's righteousness, and there will be blessings that will follow.

Matthew 6:33; Romans 8:37; Luke 18:27

Deliverance from Evil Influences

Then they cried out to the LORD in their trouble, and he delivered them from their distress.

Psalm 107:6

Today, I decree . . .

- I will not be entangled by ungodly and evil influences that are contrary to God's destiny.
- As I submit to the Lord every day, I am able to resist the devil and he flees.
- The Father is my hiding place, and He will protect me from trouble and surround me with songs of deliverance.
- I will seek God daily, and He will answer me and will deliver me from fear, anxiety, oppression, depression, stress and pain.
- I will receive the children's bread for healing, deliverance, wholeness, peace and spiritual breakthrough in every area of my life.

Psalm 32:7, 34:4; James 4:7; Mark 7:27–28

MINDSETS

Breaking Poverty

"Because the poor are plundered, because the needy groan, I will now arise," says the LORD; "I will place him in the safety for which he longs."

Psalm 12:5 ESV

Today, I decree . . .

- I am the head and not the tail, the first and not the last, above and not beneath, blessed and not cursed, and a lender and not a borrower.
- God will do exceedingly and abundantly above all that I ask or think according to the power within me.
- I am blessed and highly favored with all spiritual blessings of the Lord when I continue to walk in obedience according to Deuteronomy 28.
- I am debt-free, and God is giving me a strategy to turn my financial hardships around for my good.
- Every stronghold of poverty, lack, debt and generational curses is broken and severed by the truth of God's Word.

Ephesians 1:3; 3:20–21

The Overcomers

For everyone who has been born of God overcomes the world. And this is the victory that has overcome the world—our faith.

1 John 5:4 ESV

Today, I decree . . .

- I have the Holy Spirit's power to overcome any hindering situation, ongoing problem, unexpected circumstances and challenges that I face.
- Every victim mentality is broken off me, and I am an overcomer by the word of my testimony and by the blood of the Lamb.
- I will recover all that the enemy has stolen, and I will walk in total freedom in the Holy Spirit.
- I am more than a conqueror, and I will run through troops and leap over walls. God has given me hinds' feet to overcome any traps of the enemy.
- Even though I might walk through the valley of the shadow of death, I will fear no evil, for God is with me. His rod and staff will comfort me.

Psalm 23:4; Revelation 12:11; 1 Samuel 30:8;
Habakkuk 3:19

Leading by Example

The LORD God took the man and put him in the Garden of Eden to work it and take care of it.

Genesis 2:15

Today, I decree . . .

- The spirit of laziness, complacency, stagnation, contentment and procrastination will not overtake me in this season, but I will proactively plan my day for supernatural breakthroughs and accomplishments.
- I will command my day and write out a plan of action for success to keep me accountable, as I am a leader and not a follower.
- I will pursue passionately my God-given calling, purpose and destiny while working with others to help me fulfill it.
- I will take full responsibility over what the Lord has put in my charge to do, and every spirit of delay from the enemy is removed.
- I am not passive, and I have a purpose-driven mentality to complete what God has started in me to do in my generation.

Job 38:12; Ecclesiastes 9:10

God's Unending Love

Keep yourselves in God's love as you wait for the mercy of our Lord Jesus Christ to bring you to eternal life.

Jude 1:21

Today, I decree . . .

- I am loved of the Father and am a part of the family of God.
- The spirit of rejection and abandonment, having feelings of low self-esteem, or having feelings of being unloved, unaccepted and overlooked is not my portion. I am a child of God.
- The Lord will not abandon me as an orphan, but He will embrace me as His own, and He will comfort me in times of despair.
- The Father's love toward me is unending, unconditional and unmistakable, and I am totally free from the spirit of entitlement, loneliness and affirmation.
- I will be strong and courageous, and everywhere I place my feet God will give to me because I am His beloved.

Joshua 1:9; John 14:18–20

EMOTIONS

Godly Courage

On the day I called, you answered me; my strength of soul you increased.

Psalm 138:3 ESV

Today, I decree . . .

- The spirit of fear, anxiety, depression, oppression, anger and sadness will not invade my emotions, but joy, peace, love, boldness and gladness will be my portion.
- There will be peace within my walls and prosperity inside my fortresses, and I will walk confidently in my God everywhere I go.
- I am as bold and courageous as a lion, because God did not give me the spirit of fear, but of power and love and self-control.
- My faith will not be shaken, and I will have boldness and confidence through my faith in God.
- I will not fear man, but God alone, for He is my helper. He will protect me in times of crisis.

Psalm 122:7; 2 Timothy 1:6–7; Hebrews 13:6

No Worries

Therefore do not worry about tomorrow, for tomorrow will worry about itself. Each day has enough trouble of its own.

Matthew 6:34

Today, I decree . . .

- I will not be anxious about anything, but in every situation, by prayer and petition with thanksgiving, I will present my request to the Lord to receive my breakthrough.
- God will not put too much on me—more than I can handle—but He will give me the supernatural strength and grace to fulfill my assignments.
- I will cast all my cares upon the Lord for He cares for me, and I will not be overwhelmed by them.
- Perfect love will drive out fear in my life, and I will not take on any unnecessary burdens of my own or burdens of others.
- I will humble myself under God's mighty hand, and He will lift me up in due season if I faint not.

Philippians 4:6; 1 Peter 5:6–7; 1 John 4:18

Fear Not

Fear not, for I am with you; be not dismayed, for I am your God; I will strengthen you, I will help you, I will uphold you with my righteous right hand.

Isaiah 41:10 ESV

Today, I decree . . .

- The spirit of depression, anxiety, loneliness and suicide has no place in my heart, and I sever those unseen attacks on my mind, body and soul.
- I will walk in the peace of God and with God in everything I do.
- When I am overwhelmed and stressed, the Lord hears my cry and comes to the rescue to deliver, heal and assist me.
- I will come to the Lord whenever my heart is heavy, and the Father will give me supernatural rest and strength.
- Weeping may endure for a night, but joy will come in the morning as I seek the Father's heart and direction.

Psalm 30:5; Matthew 11:28

Controlled Anger

For anger gives a foothold to the devil.

Ephesians 4:27 NLT

Today, I decree . . .

- I will not make room for anger or rage to consume me, but I will resolve any issues that I may have with others.
- I will be quick to hear, slow to speak and slow to anger, for I am a righteous believer, and anger does not produce the righteousness of the Lord.
- The spirit of anger, bitterness, slander, brawling and every form of malice will not manifest in my life as a follower of Christ, but I will walk in the fruit of the Spirit.
- I will not sin even when I am upset, but I will walk in patience and love with others.
- I will not be impatient, prideful, unforgiving, untrusting and revengeful, but trials and tribulation will work patience in my life.

James 1:3; Galatians 5:22–26

Walking in Love

And above all these put on love, which binds everything together in perfect harmony.

Colossians 3:14 ESV

Today, I decree . . .

- I will walk in the love of Christ, for love is patient and kind, love does not envy or boast, love is not arrogant or rude. Love does not insist on its own way, it is not irritable or resentful, it does not rejoice at wrongdoing, but it rejoices with the truth.
- All that I accomplish today will be done in the spirit of love.
- I will operate in the faith, hope and love that abide in me through the Holy Spirit, and many will see God's love, which is the greatest of the three.
- The spirit of hatred, strife, jealousy, envy, competition and anger will not release offense in my atmosphere, but I will release love to cover all offense.
- I will walk in all humility, gentleness and patience, bearing with others in love.

Ephesians 4:2; 1 Corinthians 16:14

BODY (PHYSICAL HEALTH)

Biblical Dieting

Every moving thing that lives shall be food for you. And as I gave you the green plants, I give you everything.

Genesis 9:3 ESV

Today, I decree . . .

- I will be conscious about what I eat and drink and do it all for the glory of God.
- My physical body is the temple of the Holy Spirit, and I will take care of it by the healthful nutrients I give it.
- I will walk in total healing and divine health, and I will obey the Word of God concerning my diet.
- I will not just live by natural food alone, but by every spiritual one as well.
- All will go well with me and my soul, and I will be in good health, as it goes well with my soul.

3 John 1:2; 1 Corinthians 3:16; 10:31

Health and Fitness

I can do all this through him who gives me strength.

Philippians 4:13

Today, I decree . . .

- I will walk in godliness, fitness and health, which is imperative to receive healing breakthrough.
- I can do all things through Christ, who strengthens me, and I receive wholeness in every area of my life.
- The Father is dressing me with supernatural strength by His Spirit, and He is making my hands strong. I shall wait upon the Lord, receive renewed strength and mount up on eagles' wings. I will run and not become weary. I will walk and not faint.
- I will press toward the mark of the high calling in Christ and will run my race with all perseverance that I may not be disqualified.
- I will present my body before the Lord as a living sacrifice, which is my reasonable service.

Romans 12:1; Proverbs 31:17; Isaiah 40:31

Rest and Relaxation

I will both lay me down in peace, and sleep: for thou, Lord, only makest me dwell in safety.

Psalm 4:8 KJV

Today, I decree . . .

- I will get the necessary rest required to accomplish what I am called to do for Christ.
- I will regroup, reset and recalibrate when I am guided by the Holy Spirit to receive renewed strength and divine focus.
- I will make sure I find a place of solidarity and peace so that I am able to hear the voice of God clearly for revelation and understanding.
- Rest and relaxation will become a part of my daily routine to experience spiritual maturation, development and breakthrough.
- My yoke is easy, and my burden becomes lighter when I put my trust in the Lord. I find refuge in His presence, and He gives me rest from all my troubles.

Matthew 11:28–30; Exodus 33:14

CITY, COUNTRY
AND COMMUNITY

Honor Authority

Honor everyone. Love the brotherhood. Fear God. Honor the emperor.

1 Peter 2:17 ESV

Today, I decree . . .

- My supplications, prayers, intercession and thanksgiving will be made for all people who are in high positions so that they may lead a peaceful and quiet life, godly and dignified in every way.
- Revival and an awakening will happen in my city and community, and the Gospel of Jesus will compel many to give their lives to Him.
- I will not resist governing authorities, because God has established them. I will pray that He will put righteous leadership in position.
- When the righteous rule, the people will rejoice and become great, and there will be liberty, healing and order.
- If we as God's people who are called by His name will humble ourselves, pray, seek His face and turn from our wicked ways, then our Lord will hear from heaven, He will forgive our sins, and He will heal our lands.

2 Chronicles 7:14; Proverbs 29:2; 1 Timothy 2:2

God's Business Plan

For we are God's fellow workers. You are God's field, God's building.

1 Corinthians 3:9 ESV

Today, I decree . . .

- God is sending the right partnerships, sponsorships, investments and benefactors in this season that will bring immeasurable favor and increase to my business.
- What I do for Christ will last, and my business will thrive in times of economic uncertainty, famine and crisis.
- Supernatural provision and creativity will create wealth and godly success, and it will provide all my business needs according to His riches in glory.
- The Lord is sending people who have innovative business minds to walk with me and be in agreement with the business plan and vision God gave me.
- The wealth of the wicked is being confiscated and transferred to me for financial breakthrough in every area of my business ventures.

Proverbs 13:22; Philippians 4:19

Grace and Knowledge

But grow in the grace and knowledge of our Lord and Savior Jesus Christ. To him be glory both now and forever! Amen.

2 Peter 3:18

Today, I decree . . .

- I will study to show myself approved unto the Lord in learning.
- I will walk in the fear of the Lord, which is the beginning of wisdom, and I will further my education to maximize my full potential in what God has called me to do.
- I will not despise education or knowledge, for I will be empowered and equipped by the Holy Spirit to receive greater opportunities.
- I will increase in learning daily and will be one who has understanding as I obtain knowledge in the call of God.
- As I read the Scripture daily, I will be inspired by God. The Bible will be profitable for teaching, for reproof, for correction and for training in righteousness in my life.

Proverbs 1:7; 2 Timothy 2:15; 3:16

Media Entertainment

Take no part in the unfruitful works of darkness, but instead expose them.

Ephesians 5:11 ESV

Today, I decree . . .

- I will renounce all ungodliness, worldly passions, desires and offers, and I will live a life surrendered to God with self-control, uprightness and peace in all things I do.
- I will walk in integrity, and the work that I do in media and entertainment will bring glory to God's name and will facilitate the Gospel being preached so that all may hear.
- I will use every media platform to represent the King and His Kingdom, and they will reflect the image of Christ in word and deed.
- I will not serve two masters, but I will serve the purposes of the Lord in my life as I use media formats so that many will give their lives to the Father.
- Being in God's courts is better than a thousand days elsewhere, and my heart will be joyful, and it will be good medicine for me.

Psalm 84:10; Proverbs 17:22

FINANCES

Financial Opportunities

May the favor of the Lord our God rest on us; establish the work of our hands for us—yes, establish the work of our hands.

Psalm 90:17

Today, I decree . . .

- The favor of the Lord will be upon me, and it will establish the work of my hands and increase breakthrough blessings as the windows of heaven open wide for me.
- The Lord is creating divine opportunities in uncommon places that will create employment for others to be blessed financially.
- I will receive double for my trouble, and whatever I put my hands to will prosper as I dedicate it to the Lord.
- Financial breakthrough, favor, raises, bonuses, incentives, increase and promotion are mine in every area of employment.
- My name is in the wind, and many are hearing it and are picking it up in the Spirit of God to bring me to the table of favor and divine opportunities.

Malachi 3:10; Isaiah 61:7; Psalm 90:17

Wise Investments

Without counsel plans fail, but with many advisers they succeed.

Proverbs 15:22 ESV

Today, I decree . . .

- I will have financial plans, goals, agendas and objectives in place for present and future stability and longevity.
- I will save and invest in what the Holy Spirit leads me to, and I will put my financial investments in the right places so that they will work for me in due season.
- I will not sow sparingly, but I will sow bountifully so that I will reap a great breakthrough return.
- I will not hide my investments, but I will plan diligently. Those plans will lead to supernatural abundance as I obey the Lord's Word.
- I will honor the Lord with my wealth and with the first fruits of all my increase, and I will not lose any of my investments.

Proverbs 3:9; 2 Corinthians 9:6

No Financial Loss

Work brings profit, but mere talk leads to poverty!

Proverbs 14:23 NLT

Today, I decree . . .

- I will be free from the love of money, and I will be content in what God has already blessed me with.
- The spirit of financial loss, thievery and lack is broken, and it will not be my portion in this season.
- I will endure financial hardship and will not put my faith in finances; instead, I will put my faith in the Lord who is my provider.
- My hard work will bring profitable results and not financial loss in this season.
- I am relieved of any financial debt, and I will pay back what I owe. I will tithe, sow and give financial seeds so that God will rebuke the devourer on my behalf.

Malachi 3:11; Hebrews 13:5; Proverbs 14:23–24

Supernatural Increase

*May the L*ORD*, the God of your ancestors, increase you a thousand times and bless you as he has promised!*

Deuteronomy 1:11

Today, I decree . . .

- As I continue to give and sow, it will be given to me in good measure, pressed down, shaken together and running over, where it will be poured into my lap.
- Jesus became poor so that I may become rich, and I will be in good health and my soul will prosper.
- I will not become weary in doing good, for at the proper time and if I do not give up, I will reap a supernatural harvest.
- I will not be destroyed due to lack of knowledge or ignorance, but I will see a divine increase of financial blessings on every side.
- God is sending me people who will sow into my life, and daily the Lord is bringing me wealth for which I did not painfully toil. He will increase and bless me a thousand times as He has promised in His Word.

Proverbs 10:22; Galatians 6:9; 2 Corinthians 8:9

Notes

Chapter 1 The Power of the Spoken Word

1. *Merriam-Webster*, s.v. "words," accessed July 29, 2021, https://www.merriam-webster.com/dictionary/words.

2. Paul Petrone, "You Speak (at Least) 7,000 Words a Day. Here's How to Make Them Count," LinkedIn, August 17, 2017, https://www.linkedin.com/business/learning/blog/career-success-tips/you-speak-at-least-7-000-words-a-day-here-s-how-to-make-them.

3. Bible Study Tools, s.v. "katartizo" (Strong's 2675), accessed July 29, 2021, https://www.biblestudytools.com/lexicons/greek/kjv/katartizo.html.

4. Bible Hub, s.v. "692.argos," accessed July 29, 2021, https://biblehub.com/greek/692.htm.

5. Bible Hub, s.v. "4550.sapros," accessed July 29, 2021, https://biblehub.com/greek/4550.htm.

6. Lindsey Horton, "The Neuroscience behind Our Words," BRM Institute, August 2019, https://brm.institute/neuroscience-behind-words/.

7. Debbie Przybylski, "The Tremendous Power of Our Words," Crosswalk.com, January 22, 2016, https://www.crosswalk.com/faith/prayer/the-tremendous-power-of-our-words.html.

Chapter 2 Power to Decree

1. Bible Hub, s.v. "562.omer," accessed July 29, 2021, https://biblehub.com/hebrew/562.htm.

2. Blue Letter Bible, s.v. "gāzar" (Strong's H1504), accessed July 29, 2021, https://www.blueletterbible.org/lexicon/h1504/kjv/wlc/0-1/.

3. *Merriam-Webster*, s.v. "declare," accessed July 29, 2021, https://www.merriam-webster.com/dictionary/declare.

4. Dictionary.com, s.v. "decree," accessed July 29, 2021, https://www.dictionary.com/browse/decree.

5. *Cambridge Dictionary*, s.v. "decree," accessed July 29, 2021, https://dictionary.cambridge.org/dictionary/english/decree.

6. Wikipedia, s.v. "verdict," accessed July 29, 2021, https://en.wikipedia.org/wiki/Verdict.

7. Mary Fairchild, "Old Testament Prophecies of Jesus," Learn Religions, October 19, 2020, https://www.learnreligions.com/prophecies-of-jesus-fulfilled-700159.

8. "What Is a 'Rhema'?" Institute in Basic Life Principles, accessed July 29, 2021, https://iblp.org/questions/what-rhema.

9. Blue Letter Bible, s.v. "shâ'al" (Strong's H7592), accessed July 29, 2021, https://www.blueletterbible.org/lexicon/h7592/vul/wlc/12-1/.

10. *Merriam-Webster*, s.v. "declare," accessed July 29, 2021, https://www.merriam-webster.com/dictionary/declare.

11. Dictionary.com, s.v. "command," accessed July 29, 2021, https://www.dictionary.com/browse/command.

Chapter 3 The Anatomy of a Breakthrough

1. BibleAsk, "How Was John the Baptist a Bridge between the Old and New Testaments?" accessed July 29, 2021, https://bibleask.org/how-was-john-the-baptist-a-bridge-between-the-old-and-new-testaments/.

2. Blue Letter Bible, s.v. "peithō" (Strong's G3982), accessed July 29, 2021, https://www.blueletterbible.org/lexicon/g3982/kjv/tr/0-1/.

3. Chad Brand, Charles Draper, and Archie England, ed., *Holman Illustrated Bible Dictionary* (Nashville: Holman Bible Publishers, 2013), 3,271.

4. Bible Study Tools, s.v. "sumphoneo" (Strong's 4856), accessed July 29, 2021, https://www.biblestudytools.com/lexicons/greek/nas/sumphoneo.html.

5. Oxford Learners Dictionaries, s.v. "align," accessed July 29, 2021, https://www.oxfordlearnersdictionaries.com/us/definition/english/align.

6. Gabe Buckley, "Homeostasis," Biology Dictionary, April 25, 2020, https://biologydictionary.net/homeostasis/.

7. *Merriam-Webster*, s.v. "announce," accessed July 29, 2021, https://www.merriam-webster.com/dictionary/announce.

Chapter 4 Dealing with Hindrances to Breakthrough

1. Blue Letter Bible, s.v. "hamartia" (Strong's G266), accessed July 29, 2021, https://www.blueletterbible.org/lexicon/g266/kjv/tr/0-1/.

2. *Merriam-Webster*, s.v. "curse," accessed July 29, 2021, https://www.merriam-webster.com/dictionary/curse.

Chapter 5 Unlocking Daily Revelation for Supernatural Breakthrough

1. Dictionary.com, s.v. "wile," accessed July 29, 2021, https://www.dictionary.com/browse/wile.

2. King James Bible Dictionary, s.v. "H1984—foolishly," accessed July 29, 2021, http://www.kingjamesbibledictionary.com/StrongsNo/H1984/foolishly.

3. Owen Walton, "Greek and Hebrew Words for Praise," Revival from These Shores, accessed July 29, 2021, http://fromtheseshores.com/greek-hebrew-words-praise/.

Chapter 6 Contending with God for Your Breakthrough in Specific Areas

1. *Merriam-WebsterDictionary*, s.v. "contend," accessed July 29, 2021, https://www.merriam-webster.com/dictionary/contend.

2. *Oxford English Dictionary*, s.v. "revoke," accessed July 29, 2021, https://www.lexico.com/en/definition/revoke.

3. *Oxford English Dictionary*, s.v. "restrict," accessed July 29, 2021, https://www.lexico.com/en/definition/restrict.

Chapter 7 Planning for Breakthrough Every Day

1. Bible Study Tools (NAS New Testament Greek Lexicon), s.v. "hupomone," accessed July 29, 2021, https://www.biblestudytools.com/lexicons/greek/nas/hupomone.html.

2. Blue Letter Bible, s.v. "tsava" (Strong's H6680), accessed July 29, 2021, https://www.blueletterbible.org/lexicon/h6680/kjv/wlc/0-1/.

Dr. Hakeem Collins is an empowerment specialist, a respected prophetic voice, a life coach and a sought-after transformational leader. He is known for his keen and accurate prophetic gifting, his breakthrough prayers and his supernatural ministry. He is the author of several books, including the bestselling *Heaven Declares*. He has been featured on many television and radio programs and networks, including Sid Roth's *It's Supernatural!*, the Word Network, GOD TV, Elijah Streams, TBN, *Atlanta Live*, *The Jim Bakker Show* and Cornerstone TV. He is a regular contributor to *Charisma* magazine and the Elijah List. Dr. Collins holds a master's degree in Christian leadership and honorary doctorates in both philosophy and divinity. He is the founder of Champions International, the Prophetic Academy and Revolution Network, which are based in Wilmington, Delaware, where he resides.

More from
Hakeem Collins

Prayer changes everything. Yet so much gets in the way of communication with our powerful and loving Creator. In this book, Hakeem Collins unveils ten keys to life-changing results that come through the art of prayer. Position yourself every day to partner with God and activate mountain-moving faith that produces supernatural outcomes.

10 Prayer Secrets